Snakes
& Snakebite
IN SOUTHERN AFRICA

Johan Marais
with Luke Kemp

*To my daughter Melissa. May she see and utilise
the opportunities that life has to offer.*

Published by Struik Nature
(an imprint of Penguin Random House SA (Pty) Ltd)
Reg. No. 1953/000441/07
Estuaries No. 4, Oxbow Crescent,
Century Avenue, Century City, 7441
PO Box 1144, Cape Town, 8000 South Africa

Visit **www.struiknature.co.za** and join the Struik Nature Club for updates,
news, events and special offers.

First published in 1999
Second edition 2014
Third edition 2024

1 3 5 7 9 10 8 6 4 2

Publisher: Pippa Parker
Managing editor: Roelien Theron
Editor: Heléne Booyens
Designer: Emily Vosloo
Cover designer: Gillian Black
Proofreader: Thea Grobbelaar

Reproduction by Studio Repro
Printed and bound in China by Golden Prosperity Industry Limited

MIX
Paper | Supporting
responsible forestry
FSC® C146541

ISBN: 978 1 77584 891 2
E-pub: 978 1 77584 892 9

Front cover: Boomslang: Luke Kemp, Green Mamba: Johan Marais
Final page: Luke Verburgt; Back cover: Johan Marais

CONTENTS

Introduction	**5**
Snakes as predators	**6**
Vision	6
Hearing and smell	7
Growth and shedding	7
Reproduction	8
Body temperature and hibernation	9
Snakes in gardens	10
Handling snakes	12
Snakebite	**13**
Snakebite symptoms	14
Dangerously venomous snakes	14
Types of venom	15
Antivenom	16
First aid	18
How to use this book	**23**
Map: Habitats of southern Africa	24
Species accounts	**25**
Adders	25
Elapids	42
Back-fanged snakes	72
Painful bites	102
Common fangless and non-venomous snakes	108
Glossary	**125**
Further reading	**125**
Index	**126**
Acknowledgements	**128**

Wolfgang Wuster

Mozambique
Spitting Cobra

INTRODUCTION

Many people are afraid of snakes. Some are so terrified that they cannot even look at pictures of snakes or watch a snake documentary on television. In fact, snakes are secretive creatures, and most species will avoid humans at all costs, quickly slithering away when confronted or disturbed. There are exceptions, such as the Puff Adder and the Gaboon Adder, which rely on camouflage to escape detection and remain very still. Yet even though many people spend their time outdoors in areas with an abundance of Puff Adders and other potentially deadly snakes, bites are infrequent. Recent research shows that, even if trodden on, most Puff Adders will not retaliate and strike, but rather remain still in their camouflaged position. The Black Mamba and some of the cobras have a reputation for being particularly aggressive and supposedly chase after people. This is a fallacy, and even deadly snakes like the Black Mamba are very quick to flee if offered the opportunity. However, if cornered or handled, snakes may well strike in self-defence, often with very serious consequences.

The recent plethora of sensational television programmes about snakes has made them much more popular; thousands of people now keep snakes as pets in southern Africa. Reptile expos have grown exponentially in recent years and a variety of imported or locally bred snakes are offered for sale, some fetching in excess of R20,000 each. The reptile pet trade has also been flooded with venomous snakes from around the world and it is not unusual to come across teenagers with collections that include potentially deadly exotic snakes. The consequences of a bite are serious, as the relevant antivenom for a foreign highly venomous snakebite is not easily available, and any bite can result in life-threatening situations or even death, not to mention legal ramifications.

There are approximately 177 species of snake in southern Africa. Nineteen species and subspecies are considered potentially deadly, and another 30 species are known to inflict serious bites that, in some cases, may result in the loss of a finger or toe. Yet despite the abundance of snakes in southern Africa, snakebites are relatively rare and, while it is difficult to obtain accurate figures, the vast majority of victims that are hospitalised will survive. It is estimated that some 4,000 people are bitten by snakes in South Africa annually, with about 800 being hospitalised. Only 10–12 deaths from snakebite occur per year in South Africa. Accurate data on the number of snakebite deaths for southern Africa are not available.

Many people mistakenly believe that after a bite from a highly venomous snake, such as a Black Mamba or Cape Cobra, the victim can die within a few minutes or even seconds. The main purpose of snake venom is to assist a snake in securing food, rather than for self-defence (with the exception of spitting snakes); snake venom is therefore not designed to kill humans. In very serious cases, the victim may die within a few hours and, although cases have been reported where death occurs within an hour, this is very unusual. It is vital to transport a snakebite victim to hospital as quickly as possible. The vast majority of victims who are hospitalised will survive.

The majority of snake species in southern Africa are harmless, like this Brown House Snake.

Luke Verburgt

5

SNAKES AS PREDATORS

Snakes are carnivores. Many rely on muscle strength to overpower their prey, either swallowing it while it is half alive or quickly wrapping a few coils around it to kill it. It is commonly believed that large constrictors like the Southern African Python crush their prey to death; however, it is rare for any bones to be broken during constriction. Constrictors seldom suffocate their prey; instead, they put pressure on the chest region of their prey and inhibit normal heart functions, thereby inducing cardiac arrest.

Many snakes have evolved venom, which is delivered via the fangs. Venom may be used in self-defence, but it is quite slow-acting, and its primary function is to immobilise and kill prey. Some venom is prey-specific and highly effective at killing certain species but may have little effect on others. Many snakes, such as the Common File Snake, are themselves highly resistant to snake venom and there are several species that prey on other highly venomous snakes, as well as harmless ones.

Snake venom is produced and stored in modified salivary glands, which are situated in the upper jaw, roughly behind the eyes and at the sides of the head. Saliva is particularly important to snakes, as they cannot chew food and usually swallow it whole. Egg-eaters are the exception – they swallow bird eggs to the neck region, where they crush the shell and swallow the contents; the remains of the egg are then regurgitated in one crushed piece.

The sections of the lower and upper jaws of snakes are loosely connected, enabling them to swallow prey much larger than their own heads. A large python has the ability to swallow a small antelope, and a 50cm egg-eater can easily cope with a chicken egg.

Vision

Snakes generally have good vision but tend to ignore stationary objects. A snake moving through the bush or along tree branches can see small objects clearly enough to avoid them. Many snakes rely on their sight, as well as smell, to catch prey; however, a snake chasing after a lizard or a frog will momentarily lose sight of its prey if the latter freezes.

Snakes do not usually attack stationary objects, and this generally applies to humans as well. People undertaking so-called record-breaking 'snake sit-ins' enter enclosures with a variety of venomous snakes and sit very still when a mamba or cobra is close, until the

Herald Snakes feed largely on frogs like this Red Toad.

Brown House Snakes are effective in controlling rodent populations.

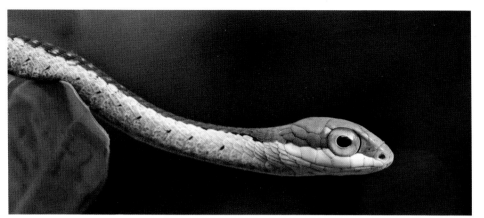
Many of the tree-living snakes, like this young Boomslang, have very good vision.

snake moves off to a safe distance. Anyone coming across a snake could freeze and it is extremely unlikely that the snake would attack. Snakes do not chase after people, and it would be quite safe to back off or run away should that be your choice.

Despite popular belief, snakes are not able to hypnotise their prey. This misconception may have originated from the fact that snakes do not have moveable eyelids and therefore cannot blink or cover their eyes.

Hearing and smell

Snakes have no external earholes and so cannot hear most airborne sound. They appear to be very sensitive to vibrations on the ground and often sense the approach of a person on foot.

The somewhat sinister forked tongue that often flickers is completely harmless and cannot sting or harm in any way – it is used for smell. Snakes, like many other reptiles, have a sensory organ in the roof of the mouth known as the Organ of Jacobson. The tongue picks up particles in the air and deposits them onto this organ, providing the snake with an idea of its immediate environment. The tongue functions extensively in locating prey and is also used by the male to find females during the mating season. Thanks to their tongue, snakes seem able to detect prey at great distances.

Snakes may also inspect dead prey with a flickering tongue, but do not lick their prey or cover it in saliva, as is often believed. When disturbed, a snake may regurgitate its meal, which would then be covered in saliva – this enables the snake to move off more rapidly, a difficult task when it has a massive meal in its stomach.

Growth and shedding

Very soon after hatching or birth, a snake will shed its skin and it continues to do so periodically throughout its life. This is because the external layer of a snake's skin does not grow; instead, each time the snake outgrows this layer it sheds it. Shedding also occurs soon after the skin is damaged.

A Brown House Snake in the process of shedding its skin

7

The entire layer of skin – from the tip of the snout to the tip of the tail, including the transparent caps that cover the eyes – is shed. In the wild, the skin is often shed in one piece, like an inverted sock; in captivity, the skin may come off in pieces, since conditions are not always ideal.

Prior to shedding, a snake's eyes become pale blue in colour – a condition commonly described as 'going into the blue'. During this time vision is impaired and the snake will often go into hiding. To begin shedding, the snake will rub its nose on a rough surface, such as a rock or branch, in order to loosen the old skin; it will then crawl out of the old skin, revealing its bright new colours. With age, the colours tend to fade.

Snakes shed according to their growth rate. The young usually shed a few days after birth; juveniles may shed more than a dozen times during the first year, and adults will shed only two or three times per year.

Reproduction

Mating takes place in late winter or spring, during which time the female will leave behind a scent trail; the males will follow the trail, picking up the scent with their forked tongue. As many as half a dozen males can be observed following a single female. Male combat is common during the mating season and results in wrestling matches, with the males trying to push one another to the ground. Some snakes, such as the Mole

Eastern Natal Green snake hatching

Snake and the Berg Adder, may also bite, and the Mole Snake will often leave very nasty wounds. Snakes appear to be immune to their species' venom and the bites seldom cause much damage.

The successful male then undergoes a mating ritual, which may include inspecting the female with his flickering tongue, rubbing his chin along the sides of the female and then twisting his tail beneath the female's in order to copulate. Males have two penises, referred to as hemipenes. Both are situated in the tail and one will protrude from the anal region prior to copulation.

The majority of snakes are oviparous, or lay eggs, and can deposit 1–60 or more soft-shelled, leathery eggs per clutch. The female will select a secluded spot, usually a hollow tree trunk, a deserted termite mound, a hole in the ground or under a rock, where the eggs will be relatively safe and not dry out. Pythons often make use of aardvark or porcupine holes. It is important that the female selects a laying site that is well protected from predators, such as monitor lizards, baboons, honey badgers and ants.

Most females lay their eggs and move on, displaying no further interest in them, but there are some exceptions. The Southern African Python coils herself around her eggs throughout incubation. She leaves only to bask outside for short periods of time, as the heat of her body assists with incubation. On her return, she will coil around her eggs again. The Spotted Skaapsteker also coils

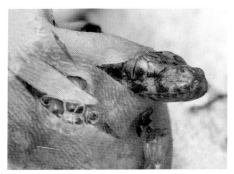

A Western Keeled Snake hatching. Note the slits in the egg created by the egg tooth.

Being ectotherms, snakes need to bask in the sun to increase their body temperature.

around her eggs, but it is not known whether she uses her body heat to aid incubation.

To aid hatching, snakes have an egg tooth or sharp projection on the tip of the premaxillary bone, which is used to cut the leathery shell from the inside. The young usually resemble the adults in appearance and will move off and start to fend for themselves. Hatchlings, once they leave their eggs, can survive off nutrient-rich yolk for several weeks while searching for their first meal.

Hatchling pythons will bask at the entrance of the burrow where they hatched, but seek the safety of their mother's coils when disturbed or after basking; this may continue for up to a month, after which they move off in different directions.

Care must be taken when a small snake is encountered, as the young of venomous species are venomous from the moment they hatch, and snakes should never be regarded as harmless just because they are small. In a recent television documentary, it was incorrectly stated that juvenile snakes are far more dangerous than the adults because they cannot control their venom and will therefore inject far more per bite than adults.

Some snakes, such as the Rinkhals, the Mole Snake, slug-eaters and most adders, are viviparous: they retain the eggs within their body until they are ready to hatch, then give birth to live young covered in a fine membrane, which is easily ruptured after a few wriggles. Snakes from colder climates tend to be viviparous, but in southern Africa there are no obvious reasons why some snakes lay eggs and others give birth to live young.

Snakes tend to be solitary, other than during the mating period; the presence of a single snake does not necessarily mean that there is a mate in the vicinity. People also often speak of a snake nest, but none of the southern African snakes builds or inhabits nests.

Body temperature and hibernation

Snakes, like most other reptiles, are ectotherms and are commonly referred to as 'cold-blooded'. This means that they have no internal mechanism to control their body temperature and rely on their immediate environment for their heat requirements.

A snake will typically bask in the sun during the early morning, until it reaches its optimum body temperature; it will then move into the shade or go into hiding. Diurnal snakes will move about throughout the day, alternately basking in the sun and seeking shelter in order to maintain an acceptable

A Herald Snake slakes its thirst at a fish pond. These small snakes are often encountered in gardens.

level of body heat to function effectively; nocturnal snakes will move around mainly at night. After sunset, snakes may bask on warm rocks to benefit from absorbed heat before retreating for the night. Nocturnal snakes also bask on tarred roads at night in order to benefit from their warmth and are often killed by passing vehicles.

In some areas, the winter temperatures drop so markedly that the snake will enter into a state of torpor. A burst of activity usually precedes this period, during which time the snake will feed regularly to build up fat reserves. It overwinters in holes in the ground, under rocks or in deserted termite mounds. On very warm days, an overwintering snake may emerge from its hideout to bask in the sun. Snakes of different species may overwinter together and, in the USA, hundreds of hibernating rattlesnakes may use the same hideout. Due to the warmer climate in southern Africa, few snakes in this region truly hibernate.

Snakes in gardens

The presence of snakes in gardens depends on locality, how developed the general area is and how 'snake-friendly' the garden is. Some snakes, such as the Brown House Snake and the Herald Snake, have adapted well to urbanisation and are commonly found in gardens. They require suitable hideouts such as rockeries, old building materials or compost heaps, as well as an adequate supply of food in the form of rodents, lizards or frogs. Unfortunately, a lot of dangerously venomous snakes, such as the Rinkhals, the Puff Adder, the Mozambique Spitting Cobra and the Snouted Cobra, are also quite often found in gardens and may pose a serious threat. Despite common misconception, there are no plants that can prevent snakes from entering a garden, nor any chemical or liquid that can successfully be used to keep them away. Snake-repellent sprays are sold from time to time, but their effectiveness has not been proven and it is unlikely that they will work.

Certain environments are more likely to attract snakes. Piles of bricks, building rubble, sheets of asbestos or corrugated tin, rockeries, compost heaps and fish ponds may attract rodents and frogs and provide suitable hideouts for snakes. Snakes seldom hide in large, open spaces, even in the dark – they prefer small holes or crevices where they can squeeze in tightly.

Tree-living snakes, such as the Boomslang, the Green Mamba and the Spotted Bush Snake, prefer areas with dense vegetation or hedges, and an abundance of food may also attract them. The proliferation of Tropical House Geckos along the east coast of southern Africa has resulted in many harmless bush snakes taking up residence in gardens, where they hide in minute crevices beneath corrugated roofs of outbuildings and are quick to disappear if disturbed. These little green snakes are harmless, but not always easily identifiable. However, the Spotted Bush Snake, in particular, is easily identified by its dark spots and bright green body.

Poultry runs and aviaries will often attract snakes in search of food. Cobras and the Mole Snake like to eat eggs and chicks, and may even take grown birds. Excess seeds may also attract rodents.

Swimming pools often act as a trap for snakes, which will swim around trying to escape, often ending up in the weir and drowning. Be careful not to handle a snake in a swimming pool – rather remove it using a swimming pool net with a long pole.

Brown House Snake

If you spot a snake in your garden, keep a safe distance of about 3m or more from it, but do not lose sight of it. Snakes disappear as quickly as they appear and, if you lose sight of a snake briefly, you may not spot it again.

There are several snake enthusiasts in cities and at least one in most towns. Keep such a person's phone number at hand, along with other emergency numbers, and immediately call to have the snake removed (or download the free African Snakebite Institute App ASI Snakes – http://bit.ly/snakebiteapp). Snakes are safely removed and released elsewhere, away from houses. In some instances, a fee may be charged for the snake remover's time and expenses, and this is money well spent.

If you are not aware of such a person in the area, try the fire department, police or SPCA. There is a likelihood that others will have been in similar situations and that one of these organisations will know of someone to assist.

Do not attempt to catch a snake, no matter how harmless or small it appears. Young venomous snakes can be just as deadly as the adults. Be particularly wary of insignificant looking snakes that are dark grey to brown in colour. Bibron's Stiletto Snake often emerges after heavy rains; it cannot be safely handled, as it has long, backward-pointing fangs and is rather bad-tempered. Should you try to handle one, it will thrash about with extended fangs; if caught behind the head, it merely twists its head to the side to stab with a fang. Its bite is extremely painful and may results in the loss of a fingertip.

There are four spitting snakes in southern Africa – the Rinkhals, Mozambique Spitting Cobra, Black Spitting Cobra and Black-necked Spitting Cobra. These snakes can effectively eject their venom up to 3m, another reason not to approach snakes unnecessarily.

KEEPING YOUR GARDEN 'SNAKE-FREE'

- Avoid storing building rubble, bricks and sheets of corrugated tin or asbestos in your garden.
- Avoid rockeries, compost heaps, fish ponds and aviaries, as they may provide a source of food or suitable hiding spots.
- Avoid thick hedges, creepers and shrubs, especially against house walls and near windows.
- Snakes prey predominantly on rodents, lizards, birds and frogs – an abundance of such prey species in a garden may lure snakes.

Handling snakes

Snakes quite frequently end up in houses and outbuildings, especially on farms and game lodges. There are a number of snake awareness and venomous snake handling courses that are presented throughout southern Africa, in which participants are taught how to handle potentially deadly snakes in an emergency situation, using appropriate tools. During these courses, individuals are taught how to remove snakes without physical contact and in a safe manner. More details are available at: **www.africansnakebiteinstitute.com**.

It is often incorrectly believed that the Puff Adder only strikes backwards.

The author safely handling a Snouted Cobra

Tubing a Black Mamba

POPULAR MYTHS BUSTED!

1. No snake will purposely attack you. Snakes lack true aggression and will attack only in self-defence. If you are more than 5m from any snake in any situation, then you are perfectly safe – no snake will approach and attack from this distance.
2. Snakes do not chase after people.
3. Snakes do not usually move around in pairs – if a snake is killed, its mate will not be in the vicinity, waiting to seek revenge.
4. Snakes cannot hypnotise their prey.
5. Puff Adders do not strike backwards, and young Puff Adders do not eat their way out of the womb.
6. The Boomslang and mambas do not drop out of trees to attack people.
7. Black Mambas do not stand in the road and strike at the windows of passing cars.
8. Snake repellents, old oil, Jeyes Fluid, coarse gravel, vibrating spikes and various plants, including Geraniums and garlic, do not keep snakes out of your garden. Rather keep your garden clear of building rubble and rock piles, where snakes may shelter or frogs and rodents may hide, providing a food source.
9. It is highly unlikely that anyone would die from a snakebite within seconds or minutes.
10. Only antivenom will treat a serious venomous snakebite successfully – snake stones, charcoal, herbal remedies, and cutting and sucking the wound have no benefits whatsoever.

Ashley Kemp

SNAKEBITE

Snakebites can be serious and sometimes life-threatening, and require swift and appropriate treatment. The majority of snakebite victims do, however, experience a full recovery without the administration of antivenom. Many are bitten by harmless snakes or by snakes with mild, non-lethal venoms. Most venomous snakes have control over their venom glands and can decide how much venom to inject when biting. In many instances, venomous snakes will bite in self-defence and inject no venom at all – such bites are referred to as dry bites.

In spite of their biting reflex, snake venom is actually ineffective for self-defence – the venom cannot kill a human in a few minutes and there would be more than enough time to fetch a stick or rock and kill the snake before the venom takes effect.

In addition, the snake requires a great deal of energy to manufacture venom and this, in turn, means that it needs food; it may therefore be reluctant to waste its venom on self-defence and most snakes would rather flee than stand their ground. Another possibility is that a potentially deadly snake may inject just a small amount of venom – far too little to cause serious damage – and, in such instances, antivenom would also not be required.

HOW TO AVOID SNAKEBITE

- Leave snakes alone and treat them with respect at all times.
- Don't handle even small snakes. Young venomous snakes are just as dangerous as the adults.
- Never tamper with a seemingly dead snake, as many have the nasty habit of playing dead when scared or threatened, only to strike out the moment an opportunity arises.
- Wear boots and thick trousers or jeans if you spend a great deal of time outdoors. Hunters, hikers, birders and fishermen should consider wearing snake gaiters that protect the lower leg.
- Step onto logs and rocks and never over them. Snakes often sun themselves while partially concealed under a log or rock.
- Never put your hands in out-of-sight places, especially when mountain climbing. Berg Adders are known to bask on small ledges and will certainly bite if a hand suddenly appears close by.
- Never walk barefoot or without a torch at night when camping or visiting facilities in the bush. Many snakes are active after sunset, and slow-moving snakes like the Puff Adder are easily trodden on.
- Do not try to kill or catch a snake if you come across one. Throwing rocks or shooting at a snake is looking for trouble. Do not attempt to catch a snake with braai tongs or pin it and grab it behind the head. Some snakes, such as Bibron's Stiletto Snake, cannot be held safely behind the head and you will certainly get bitten if you try.

A bite from Bibron's Stiletto Snake is not life-threatening, but might lead to the loss of a digit.

Luke Verburgt

13

Snakebite symptoms

Snakebite symptoms vary dramatically from bite to bite. Many snakebites take place so quickly that victims are not always certain they have actually been bitten. The severity of a bite will depend on the size and age of the victim, their general health, the site of the bite, the size and species of snake and the amount of venom injected. A bite mark is seldom the characteristic two-fang puncture mark – more frequently, a bite will be from a single fang and will just be a scratch with a little bleeding.

In the event of a snakebite, the victim may have some of the following symptoms:

- An immediate burning pain, followed by swelling, which progresses up the limb and may affect the lymph glands (the Puff Adder and the Mozambique Spitting Cobra)
- Dizziness, difficulty in swallowing and breathing, drooping eyelids and nausea (Black Mamba and the Cape Cobra)
- Bleeding from small cuts, followed by bleeding from the mucous membranes and, after several hours, severe internal bleeding (the Boomslang and the Vine Snake)
- Shock, which can cause nausea, pain and difficulty in breathing.

Mozambique Spitting Cobras account for a large number of bites each year in southern Africa.

Dangerously venomous snakes

Some 11% of the approximately 177 species of snakes in southern Africa can be considered potentially deadly and these include mambas, cobras, the Rinkhals, the Puff Adder, the Gaboon Adder, the Boomslang and the Vine Snake.

The Mozambique Spitting Cobra accounts for the vast majority of serious bites, followed by the Puff Adder, and then Bibron's Stiletto Snake and the Night Adder. The cytotoxic venom of the Mozambique Spitting Cobra and the Puff Adder causes

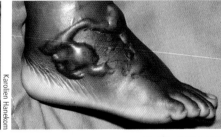

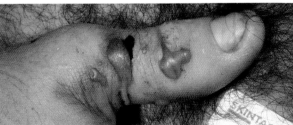

*Left: Herald Snake biting. **Top centre**: Severe bite from a Many-horned Adder. **Top right**: Mozambique Spitting Cobra bite. **Bottom**: Puff Adder bite*

14

severe pain and swelling; however, very few of the victims die – most are treated successfully, although many suffer from necrosis and even the loss of a limb. The bite of Bibron's Stiletto Snake, though very painful and often leading to the loss of a digit, is not considered life-threatening. Most of the deaths resulting from snakebite in southern Africa are a result of Cape Cobra and Black Mamba bites.

The vast majority of snakebite victims who are hospitalised soon after a bite will survive. Approximately 11% of snakebite victims will require antivenom.

Types of venom

Snake venom is complex in composition and varies dramatically from species to species. There may even be variation in the potency of venom within the same species – it appears that the venom of Cape Cobras in Botswana and Namibia is not nearly as potent as the venom of Cape Cobras in the Western Cape. There is even evidence of the venom of young from the same clutch varying dramatically.

Snake venom is generally divided into three categories based on the toxins it contains: **neurotoxins** (the mambas and several of the cobras, especially the Cape Cobra), **cytotoxins** (the Puff Adder, the Gaboon Adder and the Mozambique Spitting Cobra) and **haemotoxins** (the Boomslang and the Vine Snake). However, these are broad categorisations and don't cover all the complexities or combinations of venom – the venom of the Forest Cobra, for example, contains a mixture of both neurotoxins and cytotoxins.

Neurotoxic venom affects the nervous system. There is usually little or no pain at the site of the bite, and little or no swelling. Symptoms may include drowsiness, vomiting, sweating, blurred vision, drooping eyelids, slurred speech, a metallic taste and difficulty in swallowing and breathing. The respiratory muscles are gradually paralysed, which may lead to respiratory failure.

Ashley Kemp

Cape Cobra fang

Young female Boomslang fangs

Puff Adder fangs

Cytotoxic venom affects the cells. Symptoms include an immediate burning pain at the site of the bite, followed by local swelling that can continue for several days. In severe cases, the entire limb and adjacent lymph glands may swell. Local tissue necrosis is quite common and may require extensive surgery or even result in the loss of a limb.

Haemotoxic venom affects the blood-clotting mechanism. There is usually little or no swelling. Symptoms include oozing of blood from the bite site, headaches, confusion, nausea, vomiting and sweating. This is followed by bleeding from any small cuts the victim may already have, bleeding from the mucous membranes and, eventually, severe internal bleeding.

15

Antivenom
The development of antivenom

Antivenom was first used in 1886 and, in 1901, the first South African antivenom was produced in Pietermaritzburg in small quantities. For the next 30-odd years, although antivenom was largely imported from the Pasteur Institute in Paris, a 10ml ampoule of cobra or mamba antivenom could be purchased from Mr F. W. FitzSimons, Director of the Port Elizabeth Museum and Snake Park. A complete first-aid antivenom kit contained a lancet, ligature, syringe and two bottles of serum.

In 1928, the South African Institute for Medical Research (SAIMR) began to produce antivenom. They experimented with a variety of domestic animals for serum production, but settled on the horse, due to the large volume of blood that could be tapped during a session. Horses are made immune to snake venom by injecting small quantities of the venom at a time, gradually increasing the dosages as the horse builds up resistance to the venom. Once immunity is established, blood is drawn from the horse and the serum is separated from the red blood cells.

Rinkhals antivenom was developed in the 1940s.

Initially, antivenom production was limited to the venom of the Cape Cobra and the Puff Adder, due to the number of bites reported. Subsequently, a bivalent antivenom was produced for both species; however, this was not effective against the venom of the Gaboon Adder and other potentially deadly species. In 1938, Gaboon Adder venom was introduced into the antivenom process, and a polyvalent antivenom was created.

During the Second World War, the demand for antivenom soared due to the number of soldiers fighting in remote areas. As many as 46 horses were involved in serum production by the SAIMR. It is said that the majority of venomous snakebites during this time were to those individuals collecting snakes for the manufacture of antivenom! At this stage, the venom of the Rinkhals was added. Various monovalent and trivalent antivenoms for the three southern and east African mambas – the Black Mamba, the Green Mamba and Jameson's Mamba – were developed in the 1950s and 1960s. These were added to the polyvalent antivenom in 1971. During the 1970s, venoms of the Snouted Cobra, the Forest Cobra and the the Mozambique Spitting Cobra were also added.

A monovalent antivenom was developed for the venom of the Boomslang in 1940. This is stored by South African Vaccine Producers (SAVP), as it is produced only in small quantities since the venom yield of the Boomslang is minute and may require the milking of hundreds of Boomslangs to extract a single gram of venom. Boomslang bites are also extremely rare and the venom takes several hours to days to take effect, providing sufficient time for the antivenom to be dispatched from the SAVP in the majority of cases.

Antivenom today

South African Vaccine Producers in Johannesburg manufacture a monovalent antivenom that is effective against the venom of the Boomslang, a polyvalent antivenom that provides protection against the venom

Extracting venom from a Cape Cobra

of the Puff Adder, the Gaboon Adder, the Black and Green Mambas, the Rinkhals and all of the dangerous cobras in southern Africa, as well as a monovalent antivenom for the Saw-scaled Viper that does not occur within our range.

Vials of antivenom (10ml) can be purchased directly from SAVP. Antivenom must be refrigerated, not frozen, at 2–10°C, and any exposure to high temperatures will alter its effectiveness. Polyvalent and monovalent antivenom has a three-year shelf life; each vial has an expiry date beyond which it should not be used.

Antivenom is not a first-aid measure and, if required, should be injected by a doctor in a hospital environment. In most instances, the initial dosage will be in the region of 60–100ml and a victim may require more than 200ml. There have been instances where the victim has received more than 300ml of antivenom. The dosage depends on the amount of venom injected, rather than the weight of the victim; a child will therefore receive the same amount of antivenom as an adult.

Antivenom is manufactured mainly from horse blood – although some manufacturers use sheep or camels – and up to 40% of adults and 60% of children will experience an allergic reaction to the antivenom; in some instances this reaction can be life-threatening. Victims may experience anaphylactic shock and doctors routinely use

adrenaline to counteract the anaphylaxis. It is a popular myth that more people die from shock and anaphylaxis than from the snakebite itself. Despite the high incidence of anaphylactic shock, very few people actually die as a result. Previously, a few drops of antivenom would be injected just under the skin on the arm to check for an allergic reaction. This test is not effective and is no longer used. A single exposure to antivenom will not necessarily increase the likelihood of an allergic reaction the next time antivenom is administered.

Continuous exposure to snake venom that is spat or vaporised (exposure to venom when cleaning snake cages) may result in a person becoming hypersensitive to snake venom, causing hay fever-like symptoms such as excessive sneezing. In modern facilities, snake handlers that work with potentially deadly snakes wear masks that cover the mouth and nose in order to minimise the risk.

Antivenom should not be injected under the skin or intramuscularly – it is not effective unless it is injected intravenously and in sufficiently large quantities.

Due to the high incidence of allergic reactions, doctors are often reluctant to administer antivenom, but in serious snakebite cases it may be necessary and can certainly be life-saving.

The early administration of antivenom in severe Puff Adder and spitting cobra bites may well reduce the area of necrosis, but does not reverse tissue damage.

Vial of Polyvalent antivenom from South African Vaccine Producers

FIRST AID

What to do in a snakebite emergency

- Keep calm and act quickly and sensibly.
- Call the nearest hospital and ambulance service. Getting the patient to a medical facility as soon as possible, in a safe manner, is by far the most important first-aid measure.
- Try to identify the snake responsible, as long as there is no risk to the victim of a second bite or of someone else being bitten. Remember that the doctor will treat the symptoms irrespective of the type of snake responsible – venomous snakes often give dry bites, which contain no venom, and in such cases only the bite itself will need attention.
- Do not attempt to catch or kill the snake – rather take a photograph from a safe distance.
- Remove jewellery and tight clothing, including the victim's shoes.
- Immobilise the victim, who must lie down and be kept as still as possible. Unnecessary activity stimulates the progress of venom through the lymphatic system.
- Elevate the affected limb.
- Keep the patient calm and reassured that they will survive. This may not be easy, as people tend to panic when bitten. The victim must be taken away from the snake. Remind the victim that 99 per cent of victims who are hospitalised survive the bite. Only 10–12 snakebite deaths occur each year in South Africa – most snakebite victims live in remote areas.
- If the victim stops breathing, begin mouth-to-mouth resuscitation.
- Use a bag valve mask as required (if you have received the appropriate training).

If you are less than half an hour from the nearest hospital with a trauma unit (ICU):

- Do not carry out any first-aid measures unless the patient has breathing problems – it is more important to transport the victim to a hospital where they can receive professional treatment.

If you are a few hours away from a hospital with a trauma unit (ICU):

- Arrange to meet the ambulance en route.
- If you cannot identify the snake, apply a pressure bandage, not a tourniquet. Note, however, that pressure bandages should not be used for adder or spitting cobra bites.

What NOT to do in a snakebite emergency

- Do not cut and suck. Cutting may expose the wound to secondary infection and sucking just doesn't work. There are numerous sucking devices on the market, often available at 'outdoors' stores, but these have proved to be useless. The venom quickly attaches to the lymphatic vessels, and suction, however vigorous, cannot remove a significant amount of venom. Cutting and sucking will do far more harm than good.
- The efficacy of electrotherapy in the treatment of snakebite is a myth: electric current does not neutralise snake venom. Electric shock devices on the market will not solve the problem and are a waste of time and money.
- Do not apply a tourniquet. Snake venom is initially absorbed by the lymphatic system, not through the blood system. Tourniquets may concentrate the venom at the site of the bite, especially with cytotoxic bites, and can promote necrosis and cause severe tissue damage. A tourniquet may even result in the need to amputate if left on for too long.
- Do not apply ice or give the victim alcohol.
- Do not panic, and aim to keep the victim calm.
- The victim must avoid excessive movement, such as walking or running. This will increase the heart rate and the possibility of the venom spreading faster.
- Do not inject antivenom as a first-aid measure. Most victims do not require antivenom and a large number of people are allergic to it and can go into anaphylactic shock. This can be life-threatening if adrenaline is not to hand.

If you spend a great deal of time in the bush, ensure that you have the number of the nearest hospital and ambulance service on your cellphone. Check whether your medical aid company provides a helicopter evacuation service in medical emergencies and record the appropriate telephone numbers. For emergency medical advice for a snakebite, call the Poison Information Centre on 0861 555 777.

Pressure pad

For any unknown bite a pressure pad can be applied directly on the bite. Such a pad, made of rubber, cloth or cotton wool, measuring roughly 6 x 3 x 3cm, should be bandaged with a non-elastic bandage, as tight as one would for a sprained ankle. It can be applied anywhere on the body and may trap the venom in the bitten area and delay the rate at which it spreads and does damage.

Pressure bandages

In the event of a suspected Black Mamba or Cape Cobra bite, apply a pressure bandage to the affected limb while transporting the patient if the closest medical facility is more than half an hour away.

Do not apply a pressure bandage if there is already evidence of local swelling, or if the victim was bitten by a snake with a predominantly cytotoxic venom that may cause excessive swelling, like an adder, Mozambique Spitting Cobra or Bibron's Stiletto Snake. The purpose of the pressure bandage is to apply pressure on the lymphatic drainage system, as the venom is initially largely absorbed and transported through this system. If applied correctly, a pressure bandage may slow down the rate at which venom spreads and buy the victim some time. To apply the bandage, immobilise the affected limb and immediately apply firm pressure to the site of the bite, then wrap the bandage around the site as tightly as you would for a sprained ankle. Continue to wrap the entire limb from the bite towards the heart. For a pressure bandage to work effectively, a specific pressure of around 50–70mm Hg should be applied, and this is no easy task. It is best to use a bandage that has rectangles printed on it — the right pressure is achieved by stretching the bandage until the rectangles become squares.

To minimise movement, splint the limb. If the bite is on a leg, wrap another bandage around both legs. If there is severe swelling, loosen the bandage but do not remove it.

If the bite is on a hand or arm, straighten the arm and, once the pressure bandage has

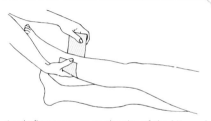

Apply firm pressure to the site of the bite and wrap the pressure bandage tightly.

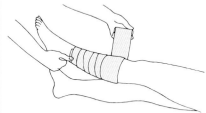

Apply the bandage from the site of the bite towards the heart.

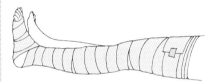

Bind the entire limb if possible.

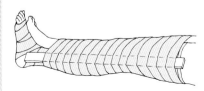

Splint the limb, wrapping the bandage around both legs to eliminate movement. Loosen the bandage if there is severe swelling, but do not remove it.

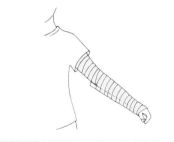

been applied, splint the arm to minimise movement.

The pressure bandage should not cut off blood circulation – if you press on a nail, there should still be signs of good capillary refill (within two seconds).

The pressure bandage should stay in place until such time as the patient reaches a medical facility and should only be removed by medical staff.

Important: Do not waste valuable time applying a pressure bandage – this can be done while the patient is being transported to the nearest medical facility.

Arterial tourniquets

Arterial tourniquets that are applied high up on a leg or arm to cut off blood circulation ARE NOT RECOMMENDED for snakebite and may lead to various complications including tissue damage, gangrene, organ failure or amputation.

In cases where Black Mamba or Cape Cobra victims are more than 90 minutes from a hospital, an arterial tourniquet might be considered but, as already mentioned, not recommended. There is little scientific evidence that arterial tourniquets are beneficial but ample evidence of them causing morbidity and even death.

Respiratory support

In serious snakebite cases with neurotoxic venom (e.g., the bite of a Cape Cobra), the patient may soon have trouble breathing – within one to three hours, or as soon as 30 minutes in rare cases. This is a very serious medical condition and respiratory support could be lifesaving. If the patient stops breathing, it is vital to start with rescue breathing immediately.

Mouth-to-mouth resuscitation may be beneficial, but a barrier device may be required if you do not know the patient. Most first-aid kits have a face mask – a smallish plastic one-way valve situated in the centre of a piece of plastic – but these are not easy to use. A pocket mask is far more effective.

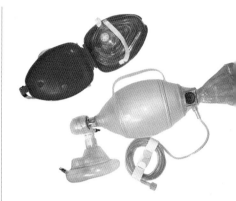

Pocket mask and resuscitator

POCKET MASK It is easy to get a good seal over the mouth and nose of a patient with a pocket mask. Rescue breathing should be provided at the rate of one breath every six seconds for adults, every three seconds for children and every two seconds for infants. Each breath must be given slowly over one second with just enough air for the chest to rise – nothing more.

If available, oxygen can be connected to the pocket mask. Oxygen may be set at 5–8 litres per minute for rescue breathing, but if a bag valve mask reserve is used, a flow of 15 litres per minute may be more beneficial.

Respiratory support via mouth-to-mouth breathing using a pocket mask is effective, but it is tiring and will be difficult to maintain for very long periods.

BAG VALVE MASK RESERVE A bag valve mask resuscitator reserve is far more effective and can be used for much longer. However, two people are required to use it effectively.

The patient must be laid on their back with a rescue breather behind the head. The patient's head must be tilted back with their chin lifted, as it moves the tongue away from the throat. The mask must have a good seal over both mouth and nose. The second rescue breather should ideally be on the side of the patient, squeezing air into their lungs every six seconds for adults, three seconds for children and two for infants. The bag must be squeezed gently over a period of one second, with just enough air to see the chest rise.

If available, oxygen can be connected to the bag valve mask and the oxygen tank set to deliver 15 litres of oxygen per minute. If oxygen is not added, remove the oxygen reservoir bag at the rear end of the bag valve mask (not required when using a micro bag valve mask, as the oxygen bag is fixed and it has a valve to allow air to enter).

It is difficult to use a bag valve mask while transporting a patient. Another complication, especially in Black Mamba bites, is saliva accumulating in the mouth as the tongue becomes paralysed and no longer functions. In such instances it is best to drain excessive saliva from the mouth using a hand pump or to lay the patient on their side to allow the saliva to drain.

Spitting snakes

The common spitting snakes in South Africa are the Mozambique Spitting Cobra and the Rinkhals. Both snakes spray their venom up to a distance of three metres and do so in self-defence to temporarily blind their attacker so that they can make a quick escape. The other spitting snakes in southern Africa are the Black Spitting Cobra, Zebra Cobra and Black-neck Spitting Cobra. These snakes can bite as well as spit, using the same venom that is spat.

Although spitting snakes aim effectively for the region of the eyes, the venom diffuses into a spray over a wide area and will get onto hair, face, arms, neck and chest.

Snake venom in the eyes

Venom in the eyes causes immediate pain and the eyes must be rinsed out with water

A Mozambique Spitting Cobra can spit its venom up to three metres.

Wolfgang Wüster

as quickly as possible. This may prove challenging, as the first reaction of the victim will be to keep their eyes closed tightly. Gently flush the eyes with copious amounts of water, ideally under a tap or even with a hosepipe. If water is not available, other bland liquids can be used to flush the eyes. Do not use milk or urine, unless there is no other option.

The victim's eyes will immediately begin tearing, which will help somewhat to rinse excess venom.

Do not use diluted antivenom. Although flushing removes excess venom, it does not neutralise it. The damage to the cornea and eyelids is virtually instant, and the victim should be transported to a medical facility. Doctors will treat the eyes with local anaesthetic, check for corneal damage and may treat the eyes with antibiotic drops or cream (e.g., Chloramphenicol) to prevent secondary infection of the damaged cornea.

If the eyes are flushed with water immediately and the victim is taken to a medical facility for treatment, the chances of permanent damage to the eyes are exceptionally remote.

Pets, farm animals and snakebite

Many dogs are bitten by snakes, usually while trying to kill snakes like the Puff Adder, Rinkhals or a cobra. Cats, on the other hand, are rarely bitten, as they are very quick and will avoid larger snakes and usually kill the smaller ones.

Farm animals such as sheep, goats, horses and cattle often suffer snakebites, usually on the face or neck, and such bites often result in severe pain, swelling and tissue damage.

There are many myths about treating animals for snakebite, but these should be disregarded. Most bites on animals are not that serious and the victim will survive. An animal that has been bitten by a venomous snake, however, must be taken to a veterinarian. In cases of severe envenomation, a veterinarian may need to administer antivenom.

If your dog or any other animal is bitten by a highly venomous snake, keep the animal

> ### MYTHS
>
> These popular myths should be discounted – they will not save the life of your pet or farm animal:
> - Forcing milk down the animal's throat.
> - Feeding it charcoal.
> - Giving the animal Allergex tablets.
> - Cutting the tip of the animal's ear to let the venom 'bleed out'.
> - Injecting an animal with petrol, supposedly to neutralise snake venom.

away from the snake, keep the animal calm and contact a veterinarian. Waste no time getting the animal proper assistance.

The bite from a snake with neurotoxic venom – such as mambas, some cobras and potentially the Rinkhals – may cause progressive weakness and difficulty breathing – a life-threatening situation. In such cases, the animal may die quickly if it doesn't receive assisted breathing and antivenom. In serious cases where antivenom is administered successfully, the recovery period may vary from a few hours to more than a day or two. Bites from snakes with predominantly cytotoxic venom – such as adders and spitting cobras or Bibron's Stiletto Snake – result in pain, swelling and blistering and may lead to tissue damage. Small animals may suffer fluid and blood loss in addition to tissue damage. When dogs are bitten in the face or throat region, the swelling may inhibit breathing; this is particularly problematic in small dogs.

For severe envenomation from a potentially deadly snake, antivenom (the same product used on humans) may be the only solution. Anything from two to six (or more) vials of polyvalent antivenom may be required. For Boomslang bites, monovalent antivenom is required, but it is not freely available and is rather expensive. For venom in the eyes, gently flush the animal's eyes with water and take the animal to a veterinarian. The practitioner will apply local anaesthetic, followed by a treatment of antibiotic drops or cream (e.g., Vigamox or Exocin). In most instances, the eyes will recover fully within a few days.

HOW TO USE THIS BOOK

This guide to snakes and snakebite in southern Africa is intended as a practical tool in the easy identification of all dangerous snakes and common harmless snakes in the region. It also aims to provide quick and practical advice on first-aid measures in the case of snakebite.

The snakes featured in this book have been grouped into five sections: the adders (pages 25–41), the elapids (pages 42–77), the back-fanged snakes (pages 78–101) snakes that give painful bites (pages 102–107) and the fangless and non-venomous snakes (pages 108–124). These are loose groupings, based on shared characteristics, although there are some anomalies, such as Bibron's Stiletto Snake (page 85), that do not fit easily into any group.

In the accounts that follow, each species is introduced by its common name, followed by its scientific name and an indication as to whether the snake is harmless, mildly venomous, dangerous or very dangerous.

Alternative common names, including those in Afrikaans, appear at the top of the left-hand column, and simple icons convey additional information about the snake.

A separate 'At a glance' column highlights each snake's most prominent features, such as body markings, diagnostic signs or behaviour. This may assist in easy identification of the species.

Colour photographs are supplied for all featured species and highlight colour variations, as well as similar or easily confused species. Maps indicate the known distribution of each snake described and this may also aid in identification. Always bear in mind that the odd snake may be relocated accidentally with goods and transported well beyond its known range.

While every effort has been made to avoid overly scientific language, some technical terms have been necessary – these are explained in the Glossary on page 125.

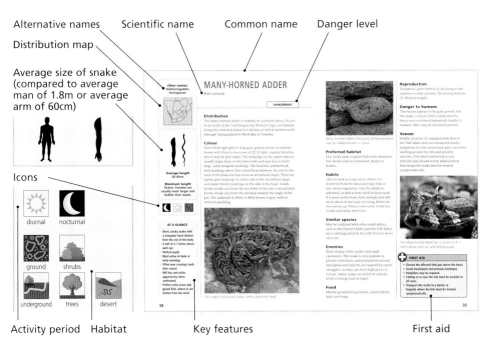

Alternative names   Scientific name   Common name   Danger level

Distribution map

Average size of snake (compared to average man of 1.8m or average arm of 60cm)

Icons

diurnal   nocturnal   ground   shrubs   underground   trees   desert

Activity period   Habitat   Key features   First aid

23

Habitats of southern Africa

Southern Africa has eight distinct habitats or vegetation types in which snakes (and other wildlife) may be found. These are depicted on the map below.

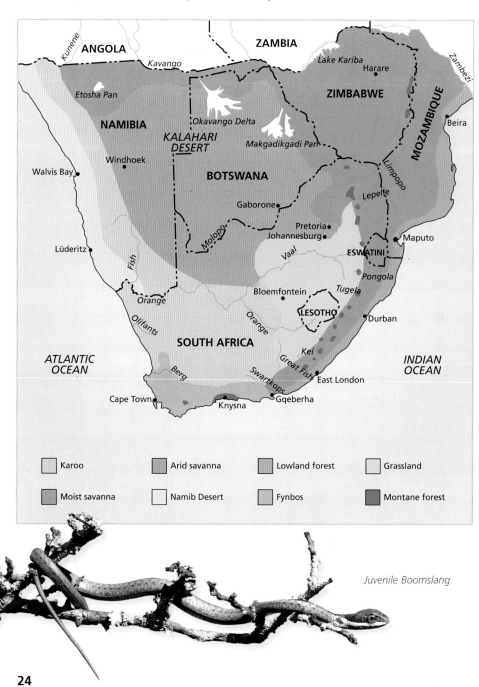

Karoo	Arid savanna	Lowland forest	Grassland
Moist savanna	Namib Desert	Fynbos	Montane forest

Juvenile Boomslang

ADDERS

Adders are very common throughout southern Africa and are found in or near most major cities.

- Usually short and stout with a rather triangular head distinct from the rest of the body and keeled body scales; the night adders are uncharacteristic in that they are more elongate and lack the distinct triangular head and roughly keeled body scales.

- Have large fangs situated in the front of the mouth. When the fangs are not in use, they fold back against the roof of the mouth, except for night adders. They are hollow and the venom passes down the centre of each fang.

- Most adders have predominantly cytotoxic venom.

- Responsible for many of the serious snakebite cases that are reported, especially the Puff Adder.

- Produce live young, except the night adders.

Many-horned Adder

Common Night Adder

Berg Adder

Gaboon Adder

Puff Adder

Horned Adder

PUFF ADDER
Bitis arietans arietans

VERY DANGEROUS

Average length
80–100cm

Maximum length
1.25m in southern Africa,
close to 2m elsewhere
in Africa

Distribution
Generally widespread in southern Africa, including the Karoo and the Albany thickets, but excluding areas of dense forest, true desert and high mountaintops. Puff Adders appear to largely be absent from the greater Johannesburg area as well as much of Lesotho and the coastal regions of Namibia.

Colour
The back or dorsal surface is extremely variable, ranging from bright to dull yellow, light brown or grey with distinct alternating light and dark, backward-pointing chevrons on the back and bands on the tail. A bright to dull yellow or off-white stripe between or slightly behind the eyes separates two dark blotches, one on the crown of the head and the other above the snout. The side of the head has two dark, oblique bands, one roughly below the eye and the other further back, extending from behind the eye down to the back of the jaw and head. The underside is yellowish white to grey with dark blotches.

Preferred habitat
This snake is found in a wide variety of habitats including savanna, grassland, desert, thicket and fynbos, where it tends to favour bushy cover and is well camouflaged.

AT A GLANCE

- Short, stubby snake with a triangular head distinct from the body
- Yellow to white stripe between the eyes
- Vertical pupils
- Yellow to grey-brown with distinct backward-pointing chevrons on the back
- Strongly keeled body scales
- May hiss or puff when disturbed
- Usually found on the ground
- Very active after sunset

These snakes are well camouflaged and blend with their environment.

26

A Puff Adder draws its head back, ready to strike.

Habits

A slow-moving snake, usually found on the ground or in low shrubs, where it may bask in the sun; rarely found in trees. This snake relies on its camouflage to avoid danger and will remain still even when approached. If threatened, it may be bad-tempered, hissing and puffing, and drawing its head back quickly into a striking position. Further harassment may result in the head dropping and this is a clear indication that it is ready to strike.

Mainly active at night and often basks on or crosses tarred roads; many are killed by vehicles. It is also fond of basking during the day and is a good swimmer.

The Puff Adder is an ambush hunter and may spend several days or even weeks in an ambush position, waiting for prey to pass. This snake may hold onto its prey; however, since rodents bite back, larger rodents are usually bitten and immediately left to run off and die; the snake then follows the scent with a flickering tongue and the prey is usually swallowed head first.

Similar species

This common adder may be confused with the Gaboon Adder, which has a limited range in southern Africa, or with some of the other small adders, such as the Berg Adder or Horned Adder. None of the harmless southern African snakes resemble the Puff Adder closely.

Enemies

Man, warthogs, birds of prey and a variety of snakes, such as the Snouted and Cape cobras.

Food

Feeds on rats, mice and other small, terrestrial mammals, as well as birds, lizards, frogs and occasionally other snakes. Juveniles are fond of toads.

Reproduction

Viviparous, gives birth to 20–40 young in late summer, but clutches can be much larger. The young measure 15–20cm in length and are perfect replicas of the adults. Receptive females produce a pheromone that attracts males and several males may follow a single female. Males are known to engage in combat during the mating season

Luke Kemp

Puff Adders are efficient at controlling rodent populations.

27

and will twist around each other and try to wrestle their opponent to the ground. There are limited records of hybridisation with the Gaboon Adder.

Danger to humans

It is fortunate that this common, widespread, sluggish snake relies on camouflage to escape danger and, when concealed, is extremely reluctant to bite. Most bites occur in the evening or at night when on the move. It has very long fangs, up to 18mm, and potent predominantly cytotoxic venom. The Puff Adder is second only to the Mozambique Spitting Cobra in the number of serious snakebites inflicted in southern Africa; however, relatively few bites prove fatal. This is largely a result of the slow-acting venom, which gives victims enough time for hospitalisation and treatment.

Venom

A potent cytotoxic venom with a degree of haemotoxicity. Other than immediate shock, symptoms may include extreme pain, excessive swelling of the bitten limb and part of the trunk. Internal bleeding often results in areas of the bitten limb turning reddish. Blistering at the site of the bite often occurs, followed by necrosis, especially for bites on the hands or feet. This may result in amputation. There is always a danger of compartment syndrome, where severe

Sluggish and slow, this adder often moves in a caterpillar-like fashion.

swelling may reduce blood flow to limbs and lead to severe necrosis, accelerated by secondary infection. The majority of victims are bitten on the lower leg or hand.

It is fortunate that the venom is usually slow-acting and, if left untreated or treatment is not successful, will take 24 hours or longer to result in death. It is uncommon for victims to die before this. Where bites prove fatal, the victim usually succumbs to complications associated with extensive organ failure. Polyvalent antivenom may be required in serious cases and should be administered soon after the bite.

Large hinged fangs

 FIRST AID

- Immobilise and reassure the victim, who must lie down and be kept as still as possible.
- Elevate the affected limb just above the heart.
- Loosen tight clothing and remove items such as jewellery and watches.
- Avoid tourniquets, pressure bandages, heat or ice.
- Transport promptly to a hospital.

Other names:
Gaboenadder,
Skoenlapperadder

GABOON ADDER

Bitis gabonica

VERY DANGEROUS

Distribution

Occurs from Mtunzini in coastal northern KwaZulu-Natal northwards to Mozambique, with a separate population found in the coastal forests and tea plantations of Zimbabwe and adjacent Mozambique. This snake is particularly abundant in the Honde and Pungwe valleys, on Stapleford Forest Reserve and in the Rusitu valley in the Chimanimani Mountains in Zimbabwe. Extends northwards into Tanzania, Kenya and South Sudan, and to Nigeria in the west. More than 200 individuals were removed from the Dukuduku Forest and released at Mtunzini, south of Richards Bay, in an attempt at preservation, and sightings of Gaboon Adders are now often reported there. Very little is known about the distribution of this snake in Mozambique.

Average length
90–120cm

Maximum length
1.47m in southern Africa,
close to 2m elsewhere
in Africa

Colour

The body is beautifully coloured with shades of dark and light brown, buff, purple and pink. A broad, buff band extends down the centre of the back and is broken up by evenly spaced, dark brown hourglass markings. The flanks are covered with complex buff, light and dark brown, and purple markings. Black-edged, purple to dark brown triangles jut from the belly on either side, with light and dark markings above, including dark brown, butterfly-like markings. The head is buff to chestnut with a dark

AT A GLANCE

- Large-bodied snake with a triangular head distinct from the body
- Pale head with a dark central line
- Vertical pupils
- Small, horn-like scales above the nostrils
- Coloration varied: shades of dark and light brown, buff, purple and pink
- Huffs and puffs a great deal when disturbed
- Always found on the ground
- Mainly active at night
- Fond of basking

The Gaboon Adder is the largest adder in southern Africa.

Two dark markings run from the eye to the jaw.

brown median line; another dark brown marking triangulates from the eye to the angle of the jaw. These complex colours and markings provide excellent camouflage.

Preferred habitat
In South Africa and Mozambique, the Gaboon Adder prefers forest and forest fringes, coastal dunes and moist, thickly wooded lowland areas. In eastern Zimbabwe, it is found in montane forest; however, much of its former habitat has been converted to tea plantations and forestry areas.

Habits
Though mainly active at night, the Gaboon Adder can be found basking on the forest floor or the fringes of forests, where it is usually partially buried in leaf litter and extremely difficult to spot. Individuals may be encountered crossing the roads near St Lucia and in Monzi; many are killed by vehicles. The Gaboon Adder population has dropped dramatically due to destruction of habitat by squatter communities, especially in the vicinity of the Dukuduku Forest; however, in eastern Zimbabwe, they appear more numerous where patches of forest habitat remain, even on tea plantations.

This well-camouflaged snake is extremely sluggish and may remain in one position for several weeks. When threatened, it raises the forepart of the body and emits long, drawn-out hisses. It is very reluctant to strike and

bites are rare in South Africa. As a result, they are often free-handled by snake enthusiasts, a rather dangerous practice with serious implications should the snake bite.

May hunt from dusk onwards, but is more prone to wait in ambush for its prey. Unlike the Puff Adder, it tends to hang onto its prey while the venom takes effect. The venom of the Gaboon Adder is potently cytotoxic and takes effect quickly.

Similar species
May be confused with the Puff Adder, but is much more colourfully patterned. Due to its limited range in southern Africa, it is seldom encountered.

Enemies
Man and small mammalian carnivores. Much of its habitat has been destroyed in northern KwaZulu-Natal and Zimbabwe. Individuals are often captured by snake enthusiasts, mainly when crossing roads at night.

Food
Rodents, hares, ground birds and frogs. Small monkeys, mongooses and duikers are also seized and there have been reports of domestic cats being taken.

Reproduction
Viviparous. In southern Africa, this snake gives birth to 8–43 young in late summer and the young measure 25–34cm in length.

The colours of the Gaboon Adder provide excellent camouflage.

Further north, the size of the clutch increases and the young are larger in size. Mating takes place during winter and spring, when the males become more active, seeking females. Males are known to engage in combat with other males. There are limited records of hybridisation with the Puff Adder.

Danger to humans

Extremely dangerous due to its size and potent venom. The venom yield is massive and, with fangs growing up to 40mm in length, a bite from this snake can be life-threatening and requires urgent hospitalisation. The Gaboon Adder is rarely encountered, and bites are virtually unheard of in South Africa.

Venom

The venom of the Gaboon Adder is potently cytotoxic and haemotoxic, comparable to that of the Puff Adder, but it may be injected in much larger quantities due to the size of the snake. Bites are extremely painful and may be accompanied by swelling, blistering and bleeding. There is always a danger of compartment syndrome, where severe swelling may reduce blood flow to the limbs and cause multiple organ failure. Polyvalent antivenom is effective if administered intravenously and in large dosages. Secondary infection may lead to necrosis.

Distinct patterning is characteristic of this species.

 FIRST AID

- Immobilise and reassure the victim, who must lie down and be kept as still as possible.
- Elevate the affected limb just above the heart.
- Loosen tight clothing and remove items such as jewellery.
- Avoid tourniquet, pressure bandages, heat or ice.
- Transport promptly to a hospital.

BERG ADDER

Bitis atropos

DANGEROUS

Average length
30–40cm

Maximum length
60cm

AT A GLANCE

- Triangular head distinct from the rest of the body
- Vertical pupils
- Lacks chevron markings of the Puff Adder
- Much shorter than most Puff Adders
- Strongly keeled body scales
- Likes to bask in the sun
- Hisses loudly when disturbed
- Strikes readily, even when the aggressor is well out of reach

Distribution

There are at least four distinct populations of Berg Adder:

- On Table Mountain and at sea level in Betty's Bay, extending along the Cape Fold mountains to near Grahamstown
- The KwaZulu-Natal Drakensberg into adjacent Lesotho, the Free State and the Eastern Cape
- The Mpumalanga and Limpopo escarpment from south-western Eswatini to north of Eswatini, inland to Belfast and further northwards to the Wolkberg in Limpopo
- The eastern highlands of Zimbabwe, above 1,500m, in the Chimanimani Mountains, the Himalaya Mountain and on the Nyanga Highlands, as well as adjacent Mozambique.

Note: It appears that these distinct populations may represent separate species.

Colour

Variable and dependent on locality, but often greyish brown to dark brown or black with a silvery-white median line on each side; this line extends from the head to the tail and is straight or wavy and may be absent. Above the line, there is a series of light-edged or orange-edged, dark brown, subtriangular or semicircular markings; below the line, there is a series of quite similar, smaller, dark brown markings that may merge with the

Typical colour of the Limpopo and Mpumalanga populations

Two pale bars extend below the eye.

Preferred habitat
Grassland and fynbos, from sea level to 3,000m in the Drakensberg. In Zimbabwe, this snake is common in montane grasslands.

Habits
A common snake and one often found basking on footpaths, among grass tufts or on rocky ridges, or sheltering under rocks. It is particularly bad-tempered and will hiss loudly and strike repeatedly at its harasser when threatened.

Similar species
May be confused with the Puff Adder, but is much shorter and can be distinguished by the lack of chevron markings and, when present, a distinct median line. Also confused with a variety of smaller adders, such as the Southern Adder, the Red Adder as well as the Common Night Adder.

Enemies
Birds of prey, other snakes and small mammals. This snake has become sought after for private collections and is regularly smuggled to Europe and the USA. Some localities in Mpumalanga and Limpopo, where they are locally abundant, are under pressure from private collectors who regularly visit. Also threatened by overgrazing and veld fires.

upper markings. The head may have a dark, arrow-shaped marking on the crown, two pale stripes on either side and, occasionally, a central, light grey stripe. The sides of the head are dark brown with a lighter, greyish stripe, extending backwards from the eye towards the jaw. A khaki to reddish-brown Berg Adder, sometimes with very little patterning, is found in Mpumalanga and Limpopo. The underside of the Berg Adder is off-white to dark grey with dark patches or slate grey to black.

Berg Adders around Lesotho and the Drakensberg are typically grey to brown.

33

Dark brown triangular and semicircular markings are prominent in specimens from the Cape.

Food

Mainly lizards and small rodents, although frogs, including rain frogs, smaller snakes and ground-living birds are also eaten. Juveniles feed mainly on toads.

Reproduction

Viviparous, gives birth to 4–16 young in summer. The young measure 9–15cm in length. More than one litter can be produced from a single mating. Mating starts before winter with males engaging in male combat, such as wrestling and biting.

Danger to humans

Berg Adders are common and strike readily if threatened or surprised. Mountain climbers are at risk, especially when placing their hands onto ledges or in crevices, where they cannot see. One human fatality has been reported, but not confirmed.

Venom

The venom differs from that of most adders as it may result in neurotoxic symptoms affecting the optic and facial nerves, causing drooping eyelids, squinting, blurred vision, dizziness and temporary loss of taste and smell. Respiratory failure may occur several hours after the bite, usually five to eight hours or more. Most patients end up on a

ventilator. Moderate cytotoxic symptoms can be expected, resulting in acute pain and some swelling, although this will be less severe than with Puff Adder bites. Necrosis has been observed in some cases. Polyvalent antivenom is not effective and should not be administered. Bites must be treated symptomatically.

Red-coloured Berg Adders are typically found in Mpumalanga and parts of Limpopo.

 FIRST AID

- Immobilise and reassure the victim, who must lie down and be kept as still as possible.
- Elevate the affected limb.
- Administer artificial respiration in the event of respiratory failure.
- Transport promptly to hospital.

34

HORNED ADDER
Bitis caudalis

Distribution
Occurs through the Karoo and Klein Karoo to the Eastern Cape and northwards into the Northern Cape, North West Province, parts of Gauteng, Limpopo, Botswana, southern Zimbabwe, Namibia and Angola.

Colour
Extremely variable: reddish (Kalahari); sandy or dark olive (Northern Cape); light, sandy-grey to orange-red (Namibia); and beautiful light and dark brown and grey pastel colours (Limpopo). There are three series of markings: a median row of grey and/or brown to dark brown or black blotches, which may be pale-edged and pale-centred; lighter markings below, which may form triangles; and broad, alternating dark and light blotches in the centre of the back, which vary from dark brown to grey, reddish, light brown or off-white. Females are often less colourful than males and their markings are often indistinct. The top of the head may be plain or have dark and light patterns; the sides of the head often have two dark markings – the first extends from the eye down to the jaw and the second from the back of the eye to the back of the jaw. The underside is uniform white to buff or yellowish white, usually with scattered dark markings on the chin and throat. May have a dark tail tip and a black-tipped

Average length
20–25cm

Maximum length
60cm

AT A GLANCE

- Short, stocky snake with a triangular head distinct from the rest of the body
- A prominent horn above each eye
- Vertical pupils
- Strongly keeled body scales
- When confronted, coils, inflates its body, hisses and strikes
- Most active at dusk
- May worm itself into loose sand with only parts of the head exposed

A Horned Adder from Limpopo with beautiful pastel colours

35

Horned Adders typically blend with the soil colour to aid in camouflage.

tongue. Juveniles are often vividly marked, with a strong contrast between the different coloured blotches.

Preferred habitat

Hot, dry, sandy regions and savannas, including gravel plains along the coast of Namibia.

Habits

The Horned Adder is fairly common in some areas and can be located by following the narrow tracks it leaves in loose sand. It is mainly active in the early evenings, but may be encountered basking during the day. Commonly crosses roads in the late afternoon

This snake usually has a black-tipped tongue.

and at night; many are killed by vehicles.

This snake seeks shelter in shrubs and under rocks and is well known for its habit of shifting into loose sand, leaving only the top of the head, the eyes and little horns exposed. This is an ideal position to escape detection and wait in ambush for prey. Known to sidewind on loose sand. When disturbed, the Horned Adder will coil, inflate its body, hiss loudly and strike repeatedly.

This snake reportedly uses its dark tail tip as a lure. Males have much longer tails than females. It usually hangs onto its prey after striking.

Similar species

The Horned Adder is easily confused with other small adders, such as the Many-horned Adder and the Plain Mountain Adder, but differs in that it usually has two prominent horns, one above each eye. It may also be confused with the Dwarf Beaked Snake and the Common Egg-eater, but these snakes have small heads with quite big scales on the head, while the scales on the head of the Horned Adder are small and numerous. Also confused with the Puff Adder, but is usually much smaller and lacks the typical chevron patterns that Puff Adders exhibit.

An individual from Limpopo showing the typical colours of the species in this region

Enemies
Predatory birds, small mammalian carnivores and other snakes. This snake is also very popular in private collections and is captured and smuggled out of the region.

Food
Mostly small lizards, small rodents, birds and frogs.

Reproduction
Viviparous, usually gives birth to 4–8 young in late summer or autumn, but this can be as many as 27. Birth roughly coincides with the time when many lizards hatch, as they provide a good source of food. The young measure 10–15cm in length and the females will grow much larger than the males. Males engage in combat during the mating season, which is in winter.

An individual from Namibia with faint markings

Danger to humans
This snake may inflict an extremely painful bite; however, the venom poses no real threat.

Venom
The venom is mildly cytotoxic if compared with that of the Puff Adder, causing swelling and acute pain, accompanied by shock and, in some instances, necrosis. A bite will not be life-threatening, but may take several weeks to heal. Polyvalent antivenom is not effective against the venom of the Horned Adder and should not be administered.

Horned Adder showing the distinct horns above each eye

A reddish individual from northern Namibia

FIRST AID
- If you are sure that a Horned Adder was responsible for the bite, get the victim to a doctor or hospital, where the bite must be treated symptomatically.
- May require painkillers.

MANY-HORNED ADDER

Bitis cornuta

DANGEROUS

Average length
30–40cm

Maximum length
54.6cm. Females are
usually much larger and
bulkier than males.

Distribution

The Many-horned Adder is endemic to southern Africa. Occurs from north of the Cederberg in the Western Cape, northwards along the coast and inland to Calvinia, as well as further north through Namaqualand to Meob Bay in Namibia.

Colour

Varies from light grey to dark grey, greyish brown or reddish brown with three to four rows of 22–31 dark, angular blotches, which may be pale-edged. The markings on the upper rows are usually larger than on the lower rows and may fuse to form large, subrectangular markings. The head has symmetrical dark markings above that extend from between the eyes to the back of the head and may form an arrowhead shape. There are lighter grey markings on either side of the arrowhead shape and darker brown markings on the side of the head. A dark brown streak runs from the eye down to the jaw; a second dark brown streak runs from the eye back towards the angle of the jaw. The underside is white to dirty brown or grey, with or without speckling.

AT A GLANCE

- Short, stocky snake with a triangular head distinct from the rest of the body
- A tuft of 4–7 horns above each eye
- Vertical pupils
- Most active at dusk or early mornings
- Often seen crossing roads after sunset
- Will hiss and strike aggressively when confronted
- Prefers rocky areas and gravel flats, where it can shelter from the wind

This snake is short and stubby with a distinctive head.

Many-horned Adders from parts of Namaqualand may be reddish brown in colour.

Preferred habitat
Dry, rocky areas or gravel flats with abundant low shrub cover in semidesert, desert or fynbos.

Habits
Likes to bask in rocky areas, where it is sheltered from the wind and may hide in low, dense vegetation. Has the ability to sidewind, as well as bury itself in loose sand. It is most active from dusk onwards, but will move about in the early morning, before the day warms up. When confronted, it will hiss loudly and strike with force.

Similar species
May be confused with other adders, such as the Horned Adder and the Puff Adder, but is distinguished by the tuft of horns above each eye.

Enemies
Birds of prey, other snakes and small mammalian carnivores. This snake is very popular in private collections, and populations around Springbok and Lüderitz are targeted by reptile smugglers, as they can fetch high prices in Europe. Many snakes are killed by vehicles while crossing roads at night.

Food
Mainly ground-living lizards, small rodents, birds and frogs.

Reproduction
Viviparous, gives birth to 5–14 young in late summer or early autumn. The young measure 13–16cm in length.

Danger to humans
The venom appears to be quite potent, but the snake's venom yield is small and the bite is not considered potentially deadly to humans. Bites may be extremely painful.

Venom
Mildly cytotoxic if compared with that of the Puff Adder and not considered deadly. Symptoms include severe local pain, excessive swelling around the bite and possibly necrosis. Polyvalent antivenom is not effective and should not be administered. Bites from this snake must be treated symptomatically.

The Many-horned Adder has a cluster of 4–7 horns above each eye and vertical pupils.

FIRST AID
- Elevate the affected limb just above the heart.
- Avoid tourniquets and pressure bandages.
- Painkillers may be required.
- Cutting at or near the site must be avoided at all costs.
- Transport the victim to a doctor or hospital, where the bite must be treated symptomatically.

COMMON NIGHT ADDER
Causus rhombeatus

DANGEROUS

Average length
30–60cm

Maximum length
1m

Distribution
Extends from Swellendam in the Western Cape, along the wetter, eastern part of the country, into the Eastern Cape, KwaZulu-Natal, the extreme eastern and northern Free State, Gauteng, Mpumalanga, the North West Province and Limpopo, as well as Eswatini, Mozambique, eastern Botswana, the wetter parts of Zimbabwe and throughout sub-Saharan Africa to Nigeria, Sudan and Ethiopia.

Colour
Varies from greyish to olive or light brown to pinkish brown above with a series of dark brown, sometimes light-edged, rhombic markings along the centre of the body and tail. The head has a distinct, dark brown to black V-shaped marking, which extends from between the eyes to the back of the head. The underside is pearly white to yellowish or light grey and may have mottling. Juveniles tend to have blackish bellies.

Preferred habitat
Likes damp areas in fynbos, lowland forest and moist savanna.

AT A GLANCE

- A short head with distinct dark V-marking and rounded snout
- Head covered with large scales
- Body scales slightly keeled, soft and velvety
- Medium-sized eyes with round pupils
- Dark blue to black tongue
- Favours damp localities, often close to permanent water
- Dark brown, light-edged blotches along the centre of the body

The head has a dark V-shaped marking.

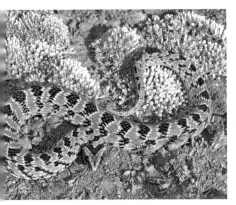

The body and tail have rhombic markings.

Habits

A docile snake that is quick to move off if given the chance. It hides in disused termite mounds, under logs and rocks, and in other suitable hiding spots, such as rockeries and building rubble. Often moves close to, and even into, farmsteads and houses in search of food, and is regularly attacked by dogs. If threatened, it will inflate its body, coil and strike aggressively. It is fond of basking and will move about on overcast days.

Similar species

May be confused with the Common Egg-eater, which has quite similar markings, but usually lacks the V-shaped marking on the head, although it may have one or two V-shaped markings on the neck region. The Common Night Adder has round pupils, while the Common Egg-eater has slit pupils.

Enemies

Other snakes, water monitors, birds of prey and small mammalian carnivores. Often killed by domestic dogs and cats.

Food

Feeds largely on toads and other frogs, such as rain frogs. May frequent houses at night to feed on toads that prey on invertebrates attracted by lights. An individual was found in KwaZulu-Natal with a bird in its stomach. Juveniles are known to eat tadpoles.

Reproduction

Oviparous, lays 12–26 eggs two or three times per season, mainly in summer. The eggs are 20–30 × 10–19mm, stick together and form a small bundle. The young measure 13–16cm in length. Night Adders are the only egg-laying members of the adder group in southern Africa.

Danger to humans

The venom appears to be relatively mild if compared with that of the Puff Adder and is not considered life-threatening. Victims may experience severe pain and swelling and can be hospitalised for a few days. There is a record of a dog of 19kg being killed by this snake.

Venom

The Common Night Adder has exceptionally long venom glands that extend about a third of the way down the sides of the body. Its venom is moderately cytotoxic, causing severe pain and swelling that may extend halfway up the limb and result in painful glands in the armpits or groin. May result in blistering but does not result in necrosis. Polyvalent antivenom is not effective and is not required. Victims may require hospitalisation, where the bite must be treated symptomatically. Not considered life-threatening.

The tongue is dark blue to black.

Luke Kemp

FIRST AID

- If you are sure that a Rhombic Night Adder was responsible for the bite, get the victim to a doctor or hospital, where the bite must be treated symptomatically.
- Painkillers may be required.

ELAPIDS

Elapids, such as cobras, mambas and the Rinkhals, are widespread throughout most of southern Africa and are often encountered. Other elapids, such as garter snakes and shield-nose snakes, are secretive and seldom seen.

- Usually long and slender.
- Have relatively short, fixed, hollow fangs in the front of the mouth.
- Have predominantly neurotoxic venom (mambas and most non-spitting cobras) or a mixture of neurotoxic and cytotoxic venom (spitting cobras and the Rinkhals).
- Responsible for the majority of serious snakebites in southern Africa (Mozambique Spitting Cobra) and account for most of the human deaths following a snakebite (Cape Cobra and Black Mamba).
- Egg-laying, except the Rinkhals.

Brown Forest Cobra

Black Mamba

Snouted Cobra

Mozambique Spitting Cobra

Cape Cobra

Rinkhals

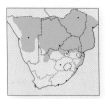

BLACK MAMBA
Dendroaspis polylepis

VERY DANGEROUS

Distribution
Extends northwards from Port St Johns in the Eastern Cape through much of KwaZulu-Natal, eastern and northern Mpumalanga, Limpopo, the northern North West Province and the extreme north of the Northern Cape, as well as Eswatini, Zimbabwe, Botswana, Namibia (excluding true desert) and further north to Senegal and Somalia. It does not occur in the Free State, the Western Cape, and Lesotho. Only just enters parts of the Eastern Cape, the Northern Cape and extreme northern Gauteng around Dinokeng.

Colour
The body is usually dark olive to greyish brown or gunmetal grey, occasional mottling can form oblique bars. Older specimens may become blackish; juveniles are pale to olive-grey. The underside is usually light grey, but may have darker mottling. The inside of the mouth is usually inky black, hence the name Black Mamba.

Preferred habitat
Found in crevices on rocky hillsides, deserted termite mounds, hollow logs and animal burrows in dry and moist savanna, bushveld and lowland forest. Juveniles spend most of their time in trees.

Average length
2.4–3m

Maximum length
4.5m, though individuals over 3.8m have not been seen in recent years. In Eswatini and Zimbabwe, it seldom exceeds 3m.

AT A GLANCE
- Large, long snake with a slender, coffin-shaped head
- Medium-sized eyes with round pupils
- Usually olive-brown to grey
- Inside of the mouth inky black
- May form a narrow hood with the mouth open when threatened
- Usually active in daytime
- At home in trees and on the ground
- Can move with up to a third of its body off the ground

Black Mambas are large, graceful snakes.

43

Short, fixed front fangs of a mamba

Habits

A large, graceful, alert and unpredictable snake. It is southern Africa's largest venomous snake and is mainly active during the day, although the odd specimen has been seen moving about at night or crossing a road. It is fond of basking, especially after a large meal, and actively hunts for prey. It may hunt from a permanent lair, to which it will return for years if not disturbed. The Black Mamba is known to share its lair with other snakes, such as the Mozambique Spitting Cobra, Boomslang and the juvenile Southern African Python. When it senses danger, it is very quick to slither into thick undergrowth or disappear into a rock crevice or animal burrow. The Black Mamba is equally at home in trees or on the ground, but prefers the latter.

Well known for its ability to move with as much as a third of its body above the ground. It is thought to be incredibly fast, but the maximum speed of any snake is probably no faster than 15km/h and only over a relatively short distance.

This intimidating snake seldom permits close approach, within 40m. If cornered or threatened, it will gape, exposing the black, inner lining of the mouth, and may spread a narrow, cobra-like hood; alternatively, the tongue will wave up and down. Any sudden movement at this stage may result in several rapid strikes, often with fatal results.

The young grow rapidly during their first year and are extremely secretive and seldom encountered.

Similar species

There is a tendency to call any dark snake a Black Mamba, irrespective of size. Juvenile Black Mambas hatch at a size of 40–60cm, so it can be assumed that a small dark snake under 30cm is not a Black Mamba. It may be confused with some of the cobras, the female or brown variation of the Boomslang, a large, dark Mole Snake or the Olive Grass Snake.

Enemies

Birds of prey, mammalian carnivores and other snakes prey on young Black Mambas. Full-grown individuals have few natural enemies. Occasionally killed by vehicles while crossing roads.

Food

Actively hunts for rodents, squirrels, hyraxes and other suitably sized mammals, such as bats and bushbabies, as well as birds and other snakes. Has been known to take blue duiker and domestic kittens.

The inside of the mouth is an inky black colour.

Reproduction

Oviparous, lays 6–17 eggs in summer, approximately 65–70 × 30–32mm. The young measure 40–60cm in length and grow very rapidly, especially during the first year, when they can reach up to 2m. Juveniles are perfect replicas of adults and are also deadly. Males regularly engage in combat during the mating season, twisting around one another and wrestling their opponent to the ground. During combat, they appear oblivious to their surroundings and may ignore people watching them.

Black Mamba hatching

A Black Mamba ready to strike

Danger to humans

One of the deadliest snakes in the world due to its size, nervous temperament, fast-acting venom and tendency to inject large quantities of venom at a time. Lacks the aggressiveness it is often ascribed and avoids danger when it has the choice.

The head is elongate and coffin-shaped.

Venom

A potent neurotoxic venom that is rapidly absorbed by body tissues. Primarily responsible for nerve paralysis, especially related to respiration, and is responsible for a number of human fatalities. The onset of symptoms is rapid and the victim experiences pins and needles around the mouth, hands and feet, as well as nausea, excessive salivation and sweating; this progresses to weakness of the legs, drooping eyelids, difficulty in swallowing and speaking, and eventually drowsiness, muscle pain that can affect the chest region and abdominal cramps. Muscle twitches are also common. In most cases, this will be followed by frothing at the mouth, paralysis and respiratory failure. Victims often mention a metallic taste. In severe cases, the victim may lose consciousness within an hour or less. Urgent hospitalisation is required and large quantities of polyvalent antivenom may be needed to neutralise the venom. Early administrations of antivenom have proven highly effective, even in severe cases.

 FIRST AID

- Immobilise and reassure the victim, who must lie down and be kept as still as possible.
- Immediately arrange transport to a hospital.
- If medical assistance is not close by, apply a pressure bandage immediately.
- Resort to artificial respiration if necessary.

Other names:
Groenmamba

Average length 1.8m
Maximum length 2.5m

AT A GLANCE

- Robust, fairly thickset snake with an elongate, coffin-shaped head
- Medium-sized eyes with round pupils
- Bright green with light green (not yellow or white) belly
- May have the odd yellow scale
- Lacks keeled scales seen in the Boomslang.
- Spends most of its time in trees and shrubs and is very shy
- Likes to bask in the sun

GREEN MAMBA
Dendroaspis angusticeps

VERY DANGEROUS

Distribution

The extreme northeastern part of the Eastern Cape, northwards throughout most of coastal KwaZulu-Natal, into southern Mozambique, and then extending to the forests of eastern Zimbabwe, below 500m and now mainly tea estates, the adjacent Mozambique coastal plain and northwards into Tanzania and Kenya.

Note: A recent publication divided the Green Mamba into two distinct species – the Southern Green Mamba, *Dendroaspis angusticeps*, in KwaZulu-Natal, and the Eastern Green Mamba, *Dendroaspis intermedius*, in Zimbabwe, Mozambique and further north. Genetic studies are under way to clarify this position.

Colour

Bright emerald green above, sometimes with a few scattered yellow spots. The belly is pale to yellowish green. The colour may be quite dull prior to shedding and very bright immediately after. The inside of the mouth is usually white, but some individuals have darker, purplish mouths. Juveniles are green with a turquoise tinge.

Luke Kemp

Unlike the Boomslang, the Green Mamba has smooth scales.

The Green Mamba has a coffin-shaped head, as does the Black Mamba.

Preferred habitat

Coastal and swamp forest and moist savanna, and often found in tea and mango plantations and bamboo thickets.

Habits

A tree-living snake that seldom ventures to the ground, except to bask or chase its prey. Active only during daylight hours, but is seldom seen, largely due to the dense vegetation it prefers. Moves gracefully and effortlessly, quickly disappearing into the surrounding leafy background when disturbed. Often mobbed by birds, especially bulbuls. Shy and lacks the nervousness of the Black Mamba, so will rarely gape. Bites are rare, but this snake will not hesitate to strike if cornered or threatened.

Similar species

Most green snakes are mistaken for the Green Mamba, but this snake does not occur in Mpumalanga, the Kruger National Park or Eswatini. It is often confused with the green variation of the Boomslang, which has much larger eyes, as well as with the harmless

It is a large, robust snake that spends most of its life high up in trees.

Eastern and Western Natal Green Snakes, the Spotted Bush Snake and the Green Water Snake, which have white or yellow-white bellies and are more slender.

Enemies
Other snakes and man. Vast tracts of suitable habitat have been destroyed, especially along the KwaZulu-Natal coast. Green Mambas are also killed by electric security fences.

Food
Small, tree-living mammals, including bats, as well as birds and their eggs. Juveniles may also feed on lizards, such as chameleons.

Reproduction
Oviparous, lays 6–17 eggs in summer, which are 47–65 × 25–35mm. The eggs are usually deposited among decaying vegetation in a hollow tree trunk. The young measure 35–45cm in length. Mating often takes place on tree branches and the tails of the two snakes will hang down over the branches. Male combat is common in this species and the snakes intertwine their necks and bodies, as they push each other to the ground; such combat may last hours.

Juveniles have light olive-coloured eyes.

Danger to humans
Although the venom of the Green Mamba is deadly, the snake spends most of its time in trees or dense vegetation and avoids people. Bites are uncommon and are mostly inflicted on snake handlers. This snake may bite the chest or neck, as well as limbs.

Venom
A neurotoxic venom with some cytotoxic properties, as swelling may occur. The venom is similar to that of the Black Mamba, but appears to be less potent and is injected in smaller quantities. A bite is still very serious and should be treated as such. The symptoms are very similar to those of a Black Mamba bite. Polyvalent antivenom is effective against the venom of this snake.

The harmless Natal Green Snake is often confused with the Green Mamba.

FIRST AID

- Immobilise and reassure the victim, who must lie down and remain as still as possible.
- Immediately arrange transport to a hospital.
- If medical assistance is not close by, apply a pressure bandage immediately.
- Resort to artificial respiration if necessary.

Note the elongate head and small eye.

Other names:
Kaapse Kobra,
Koperkapel, Geelslang

Average length 1.2m
Maximum length 2.3m

AT A GLANCE

- Medium-sized, slender cobra with broad head
- Body colour variable, from black to brown, orange, yellow or mottled
- Dorsal scales are smooth and shiny
- Juveniles mostly have a broad, dark band on the chest
- When confronted, stands its ground and spreads a broad hood, but does not spit
- Active during the day and early evenings
- Occurs in the southwestern parts of the region (few other cobras occur within this snake's range)

CAPE COBRA
Naja nivea

VERY DANGEROUS

Distribution
Endemic to southern Africa, occurring from the southern and Eastern Cape into the western half of the Free State, Northern Cape, North West Province, southwestern Botswana and the southern half of Namibia.

Colour
Extremely variable and ranges from sandy brown to dark brown, light yellow to bright or golden yellow, orange, reddish brown or black, although it is mainly known for its yellow variation. May have speckling. Juveniles usually have one or two broad dark bands on the throat that are visible when the hood is spread.

Preferred habitat
Karoo scrub and arid savanna; also found in fynbos, where it inhabits rodent burrows, disused termite mounds and rock crevices. Frequently found near homes, especially in the Karoo. It also inhabits partially developed suburban and squatter communities, where it may enter houses and outbuildings to escape the heat of the day.

Luke Kemp

Young Cape Cobras are typically light with a dark bar on the throat.

49

A pale speckled Cape Cobra from the Western Cape

Juvenile Cape Cobra showing the dark band on the throat

Habits

The Cape Cobra is active largely during the day, but is also known to forage for food in the evenings on hot days. It is mainly terrestrial, but may venture into shrubs. Well known for raiding the nests of Sociable Weavers, it preys on fledglings and eggs, and this behaviour is often observed in the Kgalagadi Transfrontier Park. Will frequently bask close to a hole and may have a permanent lair.

A nervous snake that will avoid confrontation where possible. When easy escape is not achievable, it will spread an impressive, broad hood and strike readily. It does not have the ability to spit its venom. If the aggressor stands still, the snake will soon drop to the ground and move away, but will snap back into a defensive pose quickly, if it detects subsequent movement.

Responsible for most of the stock losses blamed on the Spotted Skaapsteker.

Similar species

The Cape Cobra varies in colour throughout its range and may be confused with a variety of other snakes, including other cobras. Often mistaken for the harmless and abundant Mole Snake, as both are common and quite large.

Enemies

Other snakes, birds of prey and small mammalian carnivores, such as mongooses, as it is rather slow-moving, even when spreading a hood. Known to be cannibalistic.

Golden-brown individual from the Karoo

The Cape Cobra is quick to spread a broad hood and will strike readily if confronted.

Food

Rodents, birds, lizards and frogs, especially toads. Well known for eating other snakes, especially Mole Snakes and Puff Adders. Also known for raiding the nests of Sociable Weavers for eggs and fledgling birds.

Reproduction

Oviparous, lays 8–20 eggs in midsummer, which are 60–69 × 24–30mm. The young measure 36–40cm in length.

Danger to humans

An extremely dangerous cobra that stands its ground and bites easily if cornered. Bites are quite common and often fatal.

Venom

Highly neurotoxic and allegedly the most potent of any African cobra. Also contains cytotoxins, which cause mild swelling and occasionally blistering around the bite. As is the case with the Black Mamba and the Green Mamba, the venom of the Cape Cobra rapidly affects breathing and results in drooping eyelids, excessive salivation and sweating; victims often experience a metallic taste. Symptoms such as pain, slurred speech, vertigo and nausea have been recorded within 10 minutes of a bite. Bites are often fatal and, in the Cape provinces, this snake accounts for the most human fatalities. Polyvalent antivenom is effective against the venom of this snake.

Note the medium-sized eyes with round pupils.

FIRST AID

- Immobilise and reassure the victim, who must lie down and be kept as still as possible.
- Immediately arrange transport to a hospital.
- If medical assistance is not close by, immediately apply a pressure bandage.
- Resort to artificial respiration if necessary.

SNOUTED COBRA
Naja annulifera

VERY DANGEROUS

Average length
1.5–1.8m

Maximum length 2.5m

Distribution
Occurs from Ballito on the coast of KwaZulu-Natal northwards to Mpumalanga, northern Gauteng and the northern North West Province into Limpopo, as well as southeastern Botswana, Zimbabwe, southern Zambia, Mozambique and Eswatini.

Colour
Adults are yellowish to greyish brown, dark brown, dark purplish brown, orange or blue-black above and yellowish with dark mottling below; they tend to darken with age. The throat has a broad, dark brown band that is clearly visible when forming a hood, as well as additional scattered, darker markings. A banded variation occurs throughout the range and is more common in males; usually blue-black with 7–11 broad, yellow to yellowish-brown crossbars; the lighter crossbars are roughly half the width of the darker ones. Juveniles are yellow to greenish yellow with dark-edged scales and a broad, dark brown crossband on the throat.

Preferred habitat
Arid and moist savanna and lowveld and bushveld areas.

AT A GLANCE

- Pointed head with a prominent snout
- Dark 'tear-mark' under each eye
- Two subocular scales prevent the upper labials from entering the eye
- Usually grey-brown with yellow sides but may be banded
- Spreads an impressive broad hood when cornered, but does not spit venom
- Most active from dusk onwards
- Not found in forests
- Often raids poultry runs

Adults have brownish colouring with lighter sides.

Habits

This is one of Africa's largest cobras and has the most impressive hood of all southern African cobras. It often makes a permanent home in a termite mound or hole in the ground, where it will reside for years if not disturbed. It is active during the day and at night, foraging for food from dusk onwards, often venturing into poultry runs. It is fond of basking in the morning sun, usually near its lair, and will retreat quickly if disturbed.

Not an aggressive snake, but will assume a formidable posture if cornered. While spreading a wide, impressive hood, large adults are capable of lifting as much as half a metre of their body off the ground. Even at this stage, the snake will escape as soon as an opportunity presents itself. The Snouted Cobra is also known to play dead, like the Rinkhals.

Similar species

May be confused with some of the other cobras, such as the Cape Cobra and Anchieta's Cobra, although their distributions differ, as well as with the Black Mamba, the Mole Snake and the brown variation of the Boomslang.

Enemies

Birds of prey and small mammalian carnivores, as well as other snakes.

Food

Rodents, birds and their eggs, lizards, frogs, especially toads, and other snakes, including the Puff Adder. Also raids poultry runs.

A banded variety of the Snouted Cobra

Juvenile Snouted Cobra

Reproduction

Oviparous, lays 8–33 eggs in early summer, which are 47–60 × 25–35mm. The young average 22–34cm in length.

Danger to humans

A large cobra with a massive venom yield and capable of inflicting a very dangerous bite. When cornered, it bites readily and a full bite may require substantial quantities of antivenom.

Venom

The Snouted Cobra has a potent, predominantly neurotoxic venom that affects breathing and, in untreated cases, may cause respiratory failure and even death. Initial symptoms often include a burning pain and swelling, which may result in some blistering, caused by the moderate cytotoxins in the venom. Most victims are bitten on the lower leg and at night. Polyvalent antivenom is effective against the venom of this snake.

FIRST AID

- Immobilise and reassure the victim, who must lie down and be kept as still as possible.
- Immediately arrange transport to a hospital.
- If medical assistance is not close by, immediately apply a pressure bandage.
- Resort to artificial respiration if necessary.

Other names:
Anchieta se Kobra

ANCHIETA'S COBRA
Naja anchietae

VERY DANGEROUS

Average length
1–1.5m

Maximum length
2.5m

Distribution
Northern Namibia, southern Angola, northern Botswana, western Zambia, western Zimbabwe and southern Democratic Republic of Congo.

Colour
Two colour variations occur: a plain variation, which can be brown, orange-brown, purple-brown or very dark brown, nearly black; and a banded variation with grey-brown and yellow bands; the yellow bands are the same width as or wider than the darker bands; the throat has a broad, dark brown band, which is not always prominent. Juveniles have a dark band across the throat that fades with age.

Preferred habitat
Arid savanna and especially wooded areas along riverbanks and wetlands.

Habits
Anchieta's Cobra will often occupy the same retreat for several years if not disturbed, much like its close relative, the Snouted Cobra. It is often found near pans with water. Active during the day and at night, especially in the early evening, when it will

AT A GLANCE
- Broad head
- A pointed snout
- Two subocular scales prevent the upper labials from entering the eye
- Spreads an impressive broad hood when cornered
- Does not spit venom
- Most active from dusk onwards
- Likes to bask near its retreat
- Often found along wooded riverbanks

Scales across the back of the hood are characteristically large.

A juvenile with the dark band visible on the throat

forage for food and venture into poultry runs. When cornered, it will spread an impressive hood and bite readily; however, it will drop quickly to the ground and escape if given the opportunity. Anchieta's Cobra reportedly plays dead like the Rinkhals. This snake cannot spit its venom.

Similar species
Easily confused with other large snakes, including the Snouted Cobra, Cape Cobra, Black Mamba and the brown variation of the Boomslang.

Enemies
Birds of prey and small mammalian carnivores, as well as other snakes.

The snout is pointed.

A banded variety may also be found.

Food
Rodents, birds and their eggs, lizards, frogs and other snakes.

Reproduction
Oviparous, lays up to 33 eggs in early summer, which are 47–60 × 25–35mm. The young average 24–34cm in length.

Danger to humans
A large cobra capable of inflicting a very dangerous bite. When cornered, this snake bites readily.

Venom
A potent, predominantly neurotoxic venom, which affects breathing and, in untreated cases, may cause respiratory failure and death. Initial symptoms may include a burning pain and swelling that can result in some blistering, a result of the moderate cytotoxins in the venom. Bites from this snake are rare due to the remote areas in which it occurs. Polyvalent antivenom is effective against the venom of this snake.

 FIRST AID

- Immobilise and reassure the victim, who must lie down and remain as still as possible.
- Immediately arrange transport to a hospital.
- If medical assistance is not close by, immediately apply a pressure bandage.
- Resort to artificial respiration if necessary.

BROWN FOREST COBRA

Naja subfulva

Average length
1.5–2m

Maximum length
2.7m

VERY DANGEROUS

Distribution
Occurs from just north of Durban, northwards along the KwaZulu-Natal coast into northern Kruger National Park, the eastern tip of the Soutpansberg, as well as Mozambique, eastern Zimbabwe, Malawi, Zambia and further north.

Colour
The head, neck and forepart of the body are usually yellowish brown to dark brown and heavily flecked with black, becoming dark brown to shiny black towards the rear and tail, sometimes with speckling. The underside is creamy white to yellow, often with dark blotches. The neck may have one or more dark blotches or bands, which are visible when spreading a hood. Juveniles have up to five black bands on the throat, but these fade with age.

Preferred habitat
Usually associated with closed-canopy, coastal, lowland forest and moist savanna, where it favours coastal thickets and riverine bush. Has been found recently in thick bush near Pafuri in the north of Kruger National Park, as well as the eastern tip of the Soutpansberg.

AT A GLANCE

- A muscular snake with highly polished scales, giving it a shiny appearance
- Blunt head
- Tail section is blackish and darker than the front half
- Climbs well and is often found in or near water
- Spreads a tall, narrow hood if cornered
- Does not spit its venom.
- Prefers thickly vegetated habitats
- Active largely in the early mornings and at dusk

The rear and tail are typically much darker.

56

Stands tall and forms a narrow hood if threatened.

Habits
A large, active and alert snake that climbs well and is equally at home on land and in the water. Though primarily active at night, it is fond of basking and is often encountered during the day, especially in the mornings and afternoons. It will also hunt for food on overcast days. When disturbed, it is quick to disappear into dense thickets; if cornered, it will spread a narrow hood and bite readily. This cobra does not spit its venom.

Similar species
Often mistaken for the Black Mamba, but can be distinguished by its very shiny body scales. May also be confused with some of the larger grass snakes, as well as the Snouted Cobra and the Mozambique Spitting Cobra.

Enemies
Other snakes, birds of prey, small mammalian carnivores and crocodiles.

Food
Small mammals, birds, frogs and other snakes. It also feeds on fish.

Reproduction
Oviparous, lays 11–26 smooth, white eggs in summer, which are 46–61 × 24–32mm. The eggs stick together in a bunch – they are moist when laid and the shells are soft and leathery, causing them to adhere as they dry out. The young measure 27–40cm in length.

Danger to humans
Though extremely venomous, this retiring snake seldom bites.

Venom
Potently neurotoxic, but also known to have cytotoxic effects. Due to this snake's restricted distribution and shy nature, bites are rare in South Africa. Polyvalent antivenom is effective against the venom of this snake.

The Brown Forest Cobra appears shiny due to its highly polished scales.

FIRST AID

- Immobilise and reassure the victim, who must lie down and remain as still as possible.
- Immediately arrange transport to a hospital.
- If medical assistance is not close by, immediately apply a pressure bandage.
- Resort to artificial respiration if necessary.

BLACK SPITTING COBRA
Naja nigricincta woodi

VERY DANGEROUS

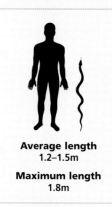

Average length
1.2–1.5m

Maximum length
1.8m

Distribution
Occurs from the Cederberg northwards to Namaqualand, and as far east as Tswalu Kalahari and the Witsand Nature Reserve, as well as southern, central and western Namibia.

Colour
Black to shiny black. Juveniles are grey with a black head.

Preferred habitat
Dry riverbeds and rocky terrain in arid areas.

Habits
A poorly known snake, often seen crossing roads and moving about in dry riverbeds. Active and alert during the day, but also at night. Usually found in rocky habitat but is also known to climb trees. Quick to flee but will stand its ground if threatened and will spit readily.

Similar species
Often mistaken for dark-coloured Cape Cobras and the Mole Snake.

Enemies
Unknown. Very popular in the pet trade, but not an easy snake to collect in numbers that would affect the species.

AT A GLANCE

- Broad head with a round snout
- Shiny pitch black with glossy belly
- Frequents dry riverbeds or rocky hills
- Active during the day and at night
- A shy snake that is quick to escape
- If cornered, readily spreads its hood and spits

Ashley Kemp

A shy snake, this cobra is quick to escape into bushes or rock crevices.

If cornered, the Black Spitting Cobra is quick to spread a hood and spit its venom.

Food
Rodents, lizards, amphibians and snakes, such as the Puff Adder.

Reproduction
Oviparous, lays 10–20 eggs, each measuring 29-37 x 17-24mm. The young measure 36–37cm.

Danger to humans
This snake rarely bites or spits, as it lives largely in remote areas and is very quick to flee when given the opportunity.

Venom
The venom is potently cytotoxic and will cause severe pain, swelling and necrosis. Polyvalent antivenom should be used in cases of severe envenomation.

Note the dark eyes.

 FIRST AID

- Immobilise and reassure the victim, who must lie down and remain as still as possible.
- Elevate the affected limb just above the heart.
- Avoid tourniquets and pressure bandages if the snake has been positively identified, as bandages will do more harm than good.
- Immediately transport the victim to hospital.
- For venom in the eyes, immediately rinse the eyes adequately with water and take the patient to a doctor for further treatment.

It is usually a shiny black colour.

BLACK-NECKED SPITTING COBRA
Naja nigricollis

VERY DANGEROUS

Average length 1.2–1.5m

Maximum length
2m in southern Africa,
but up to 2.2m in
central Africa.

AT A GLANCE

- Broad head with round snout
- Uniform black or grey to grey-brown, sometimes with reddish or pinkish marks on the black throat
- Readily spreads its hood and spits
- Often stands its ground when threatened

Distribution
In southern Africa, this snake is only found in northern Namibia and occurs further north as far as Senegal and Sudan.

Colour
Variable, but usually uniform black with reddish or pinkish markings on the throat that may encircle the neck. Elsewhere in the range, they may be brown with a lighter belly and brown bars on the neck. Juveniles are grey with a black head and neck.

Preferred habitat
Mainly moist and dry savanna, but this snake is very adaptable and may be found near houses.

Habits
Like the Mozambique Spitting Cobra, this snake is a ground-dweller, but climbs well and may be found in trees. Largely nocturnal, but known to bask and hunt during the day or will seek shelter in termite mounds, hollow tree trunks or animal holes in the ground. If threatened, it may spread a hood and can spit effectively up to a distance of 3m. This snake will spit from a reared position, but, unlike the Rinkhals, it can also spit when not reared, for example, from inside a hollow tree trunk or a rock crevice.

Black-necked Spitting Cobras are quick to spread a hood and spit.

Some specimens are brown.

Similar species
In the Caprivi, it can be mistaken for Anchieta's Cobra, the Black Mamba and the Mozambique Spitting Cobra, although only the latter spits its venom. Can be distinguished from Anchieta's Cobra by the absence of subocular scales.

Enemies
Birds of prey and small mammalian carnivores, as well as other snakes.

Food
An opportunistic hunter that feeds on rodents, birds, frogs, other snakes and lizards, including monitor lizards. Also raids poultry runs for eggs and chicks.

Reproduction
Oviparous, lays 8–20 eggs in summer, which are 25 × 40mm. The young measure 36cm in length.

Danger to humans
A large snake that bites or spits and has a potent venom; however, it is only found in a small area of southern Africa.

Venom
Largely cytotoxic and symptoms usually include severe pain and swelling, and may be followed by necrosis, blistering and tissue

The head is broad with a rounded snout. The throat is black, sometimes with some pink, orange or reddish marks.

damage. Some neurotoxic symptoms have been recorded, such as sweating, excessive salivation, drooping eyelids and difficulty in breathing. Such bites can result in severe tissue scarring and the loss of digits, and even limbs. Since this snake spits readily, victims often end up with venom in their eyes, resulting in burning pain and temporary blindness. Polyvalent antivenom should be used in cases of severe envenomation.

 FIRST AID

- Immobilise and reassure the victim, who must lie down and remain as still as possible.
- Elevate the affected limb just above the heart.
- Avoid tourniquets and pressure bandages if the snake has been positively identified, as bandages will do more harm than good.
- Immediately transport the victim to hospital.
- For venom in the eyes, immediately rinse the eyes adequately with water and take the patient to a doctor for further treatment.

ZEBRA COBRA
Naja nigricincta nigricincta

VERY DANGEROUS

Average length
1–1.2m

Maximum length
Rarely exceeds 1.8m

AT A GLANCE

- A slender snake with broad head slightly distinct from the body and a round snout
- Vivid dark rings or crossbars on the body and tail
- Readily spreads its hood and spits
- Shy; readily moves off if threatened
- Often found on roads at night, especially after rain

Distribution
The Namib Desert and Karoo regions of central and northern Namibia, extending into southern Angola.

Colour
A banded snake with 50–85 vivid black rings or crossbars on a light brown to pinkish or off-white body and up to 32 crossbars on the tail. The crossbars usually encircle the body. The throat is black to very dark brown and the head is dark brown. Individuals from Angola may be light brown with faded brown or red-brown crossbars and a dark head. The crossbars seem to fade further north and specimens from Windhoek or further south may appear black with very faint white bands.

Preferred habitat
Desert and semi-arid areas.

Habits
A nocturnal snake that is often found on tarred roads, especially after rain. It is shy, choosing to escape if it has the choice; if cornered, it will spread a hood and may bite or spit its venom. Known to frequent human dwellings and will enter houses at night.

This snake has distinct black rings or crossbars on the body and tail.

Luke Kemp

The Zebra Cobra is quick to spit if approached or threatened.

Similar species

It may be confused with the harmless tiger snakes, the darker Spotted Bush Snake of Namibia and the coral snakes.

Enemies

Birds of prey and other snakes. Many snakes are killed by vehicles while crossing roads at night.

Food

Lizards, frogs and small mammals, as well as other snakes.

Reproduction

Oviparous, lays 10–24 eggs of 29-72.9 x 17-34mm. Hatchlings measure 17-34cm.

Danger to humans

Common throughout its range and accounts for a number of bites among humans.

In Angola, this snake is often a light brown colour.

Venom

As in the case of most spitting cobras, the venom of this snake is dangerously cytotoxic and will cause severe pain, swelling and necrosis. Polyvalent antivenom should be used in cases of severe envenomation.

 FIRST AID

- Immobilise and reassure the victim, who must lie down and remain as still as possible.
- Elevate the affected limb just above the heart.
- Avoid tourniquets and pressure bandages if the snake has been positively identified; bandages will do more harm than good.
- Immediately transport the victim to hospital.
- For venom in the eyes, immediately rinse the eyes adequately with water and take the patient to a doctor for further treatment.

The head is usually a lighter brown than the body.

MOZAMBIQUE SPITTING COBRA

Naja mossambica

VERY DANGEROUS

Average length 1–1.2m
Maximum length 1.84m

Distribution
Throughout most of KwaZulu-Natal northwards to Mpumalanga, the North West Province, northern Gauteng and Limpopo, as well as Eswatini, Mozambique, Zimbabwe, eastern and northern Botswana, northeastern Namibia, southern and eastern Zambia and Tanzania, extending to Pemba in Zanzibar.

Colour
Olive-brown to slate grey with dark-edged scales; salmon pink to yellowish belly with black crossbars and blotches on a salmon pink neck, which are clearly visible when the snake spreads a hood.

Preferred habitat
Very common throughout its range. Found largely in moist savanna and lowland forest, where it favours broken, rocky ground, termite mounds, hollow logs and animal holes, often close to a permanent water source.

Habits
Mainly active at night and on overcast days, although individuals may hunt for food during the day or move about in search of water. Frequently seen crossing roads at night. Juveniles tend to

AT A GLANCE
- Medium-sized eyes with round pupils
- Slate grey to olive-brown above, with dark-edged scales
- Underside usually salmon pink or yellowish
- May spread a hood when cornered and can spit its venom
- Irregular black markings in the throat region visible when hood is spread
- May play dead

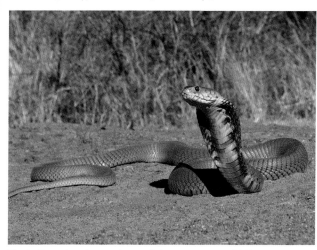

The belly and neck are salmon pink to orange or whitish.

be more active during the day. A shy, retiring snake that seldom stands its ground and is quick to flee if given the opportunity. If cornered, it may spread a hood, but will not hold the pose for long. Other than a quick escape, its main defence is to spit venom.

The fangs are specially modified for spitting: the venom canal openings near the tips are directed forwards and at right angles to the fangs, enabling the snake to eject its venom in excess of 2m. It does not always spread a hood when ejecting venom and may only open its mouth slightly when doing so. It can spit effectively from within a rock crevice. The venom supply, when spitting, is seemingly inexhaustible.

Like the Rinkhals, this snake is also known to play dead.

Similar species

May be confused with several other cobras, the Rinkhals, Reticulated Centipede-eater and the Mole Snake.

The black bars on the throat are prominent and are even noticeable when the snake is moving flat along the ground.

Enemies

Birds of prey and small mammalian carnivores, as well as other snakes.

Food

An opportunistic feeder, which will eat small mammals, birds, frogs, insects and other snakes, including the Puff Adder. May also enter poultry runs in search of eggs and chicks.

The Mozambique Spitting Cobra is a good climber.

This species spits its venom.

develop at the site of the bite within a few hours, followed by necrosis and blistering several days later. Only mild neurotoxic symptoms such as drowsiness occur, and deaths are rare. Many victims suffer multiple bites while sleeping at night. Early administration of polyvalent antivenom may reduce the extent of tissue damage. As this snake spits readily, victims often end up with venom in their eyes, resulting in immediate burning pain and temporary blindness.

The eyes are light brown with a round pupil.

Juveniles are often lighter in colour than the adults.

Reproduction
Oviparous, lays 10–22 eggs in midsummer, which are 35 × 20mm. The young measure 23–25cm in length.

Danger to humans
A common snake with a potent venom that accounts for the majority of serious snakebites in southern Africa, especially in KwaZulu-Natal, Mpumalanga and Eswatini. Commonly enters huts where people are sleeping on the floor and is known to bite exposed skin seemingly in a feeding response. If venom lands on the hair, face, arms or elsewhere on the body, it poses no great threat; venom in the eyes causes an immediate burning sensation.

Venom
The venom is predominantly and potently cytotoxic, causing a lot of pain, swelling and serious tissue damage, which may require skin grafts. Swelling often involves the entire limb and may spread to the trunk. Dark areas

FIRST AID
- Immobilise and reassure the victim, who must lie down and remain as still as possible.
- Elevate the affected limb just above the heart.
- Avoid tourniquets and pressure bandages if the snake has been positively identified; bandages will do more harm than good.
- Immediately transport the patient to hospital.
- For venom in the eyes, immediately rinse the eyes adequately with water, and take the victim to a doctor for further treatment.

Average length
1m

Maximum length
1.5m

AT A GLANCE

- Strongly keeled scales on body and tail
- Usually has a black belly and white bars on the throat
- May have bands on the body
- Lifts its body and spreads a broad hood when confronted
- Can spit its venom
- Largely active during the day
- May feign death
- Likes to bask in morning sun

RINKHALS
Hemachatus haemachatus

(VERY DANGEROUS)

Distribution
Occurs from sea level in the Western Cape, close to Cape Town, eastwards into the Eastern Cape and northwards along the eastern escarpment throughout the grasslands of KwaZulu-Natal into Mpumalanga, the eastern Free State, Gauteng and the eastern North West Province, as well as western Eswatini and Lesotho. The population in Nyanga National Park in eastern Zimbabwe is now considered a separate species based on genetics, but has not been seen since the 1980s.

Colour
Grey-black to olive or dark brown with one or two, rarely three, white bands on the throat, which are more visible when the hood is spread, especially in Gauteng and the Free State. In the KwaZulu-Natal midlands, the Eastern Cape, and southern Cape, the Rinkhals has thin bands on the body, which are creamy white or yellow to yellow-orange. The underside is dark brown to black, often with pale edges.

Preferred habitat
Grassland, moist savanna, lowland forest and fynbos. This snake is often found on smallholdings, especially in the greater Johannesburg region.

On the Highveld, the Rinkhals is dark in colour with one or two white bands on the throat.

67

This snake will play dead, sometimes twisting its body upside down, when approached.

Habits

Although this snake resembles a cobra, it is not a true cobra. Cobras are egg-layers and have smooth body scales, while the Rinkhals gives birth to live young and has keeled body scales. There are also some skeletal differences.

The Rinkhals is quite common throughout most of its range, especially in the grasslands of the higher-lying areas. Despite extensive urban development, it is still common in parts of the greater Johannesburg area, especially near vleis, dams, compost

Rinkhals in the southern and eastern parts of the range are often banded with yellow or orange on the back.

Luke Kemp

heaps, stables and rockeries. Some individuals live in rockeries right next to major highways.

This snake is very effective at regulating its body temperature and is fond of basking on hot days in the middle of winter. It is largely diurnal and basks in the morning prior to foraging. It may also be encountered hunting on summer nights. The Rinkhals is quick to flee when disturbed and often stays close to a hole or other suitable hiding place; if cornered, it will lift as much as half of its body off the ground, spread a hood and display white bands on the throat. It is a good climber and may climb into hedges and even trees, especially when attempting to escape.

This snake spits venom from an upright position, while spreading a hood; it throws the elevated part of the body forward and may hiss at the same time. It will aim at the aggressor's eyes and can eject venom from up to 2m away.

If approached closely, the Rinkhals may drop to the ground and play dead, twisting the anterior part of its body sideways or even upside down, with the mouth open and the tongue hanging out. If picked up, it may hang limply or strike out unexpectedly.

Human bites are very rare, but dogs and farm animals are often bitten, although the venom is not potent enough to kill larger animals, such as horses.

Similar species
May be confused with a variety of harmless snakes, such as the Mole Snake, as well as with the Mozambique Spitting Cobra and the Snouted Cobra.

Enemies
Other snakes and birds of prey are major predators, but many are killed by dogs and people. Destruction of habitat due to urban development poses the biggest threat.

Food
Very partial to toads, but also feeds on lizards, rodents, snakes, birds and their eggs. The eggs are swallowed whole.

Reproduction
Viviparous, gives birth to 20–30 live young in late summer, but this can be as many as 63. The young average 16–22cm in length and resemble the adults in appearance.

Rinkhals will stand tall with a broad hood if threatened.

Young Rinkhals in the Highveld are often grey to brown, becoming darker as they age.

Danger to humans
This snake spits and bites. Its venom is potentially deadly, but not as potent as that of most cobras. Human fatalities are virtually unheard of.

Venom
A cytotoxic and neurotoxic venom that causes painful swelling of the affected limb and often necrosis at the site of the bite. Other symptoms may include nausea, dizziness and respiratory distress. Polyvalent antivenom is effective against the venom of this snake.

 FIRST AID

- Immobilise and reassure the victim, who must lie down and remain as still as possible.
- Elevate the affected limb just above the heart.
- Avoid tourniquets and pressure bandages if the snake has been positively identified; bandages will do more harm than good.
- Immediately transport the victim to hospital.
- For venom in the eyes, immediately rinse the eyes adequately with water and take the patient to a doctor for further treatment.

CAPE CORAL SNAKE

Aspidelaps lubricus lubricus

DANGEROUS

Average length
30–60cm

Maximum length
60cm

Distribution
The Cape Coral Snake occurs from near Somerset East and Port Elizabeth in the east, westwards to Cape Town and northwards into southern Namibia, as well as the northern Eastern Cape and the south-western Free State.

Colour
The Cape Coral Snake is orange-yellow to coral-red above with 20–47 well-defined, narrow, black or dark brown crossbars, which may encircle the body and tail. There is a short, vertical black stripe from the eye to the mouth that usually extends between the eyes on the head. The belly is yellowish white with black crossbars.

Preferred habitat
Rocky outcrops and stony, dry, sandy regions in arid savanna, Karoo scrub, fynbos and desert.

Habits
This snake spends most of its life underground, emerging in the early evening to hunt for food. It is very active after rains and many individuals are killed on roads. It is a bad-tempered snake that spreads a narrow hood when cornered; it will strike repeatedly while hissing and lunging forward.

Similar species
Easily confused with the tiger snakes and the Zebra Cobra in Namibia.

AT A GLANCE

- A dull yellow, orange-yellow to coral red snake with darker crossbars
- Head is orange with some black markings
- Has an enlarged rostral scale
- Usually only active at night
- When threatened, rears up with a narrow hood
- Strikes repeatedly while lunging forward and hissing
- Often seen crossing roads at night

This snake is quick to rear up and form a hood when threatened.

70

Distinct dark brown or black crossbars encircle the body and tail.

Enemies
Other snakes. This snake is popular in the pet trade and is frequently targeted by reptile smugglers.

Food
Lizards, particularly legless lizards that live largely underground, small snakes, frogs and rodents. Will also eat reptile eggs.

The hood is narrow but distinct.

Reproduction
Oviparous, lays 3–11 eggs in summer, which measure 45–54mm. The young measure 17–18cm in length. Females may produce more than one clutch of eggs per season.

Danger to humans
Bites from this snake do not usually result in life-threatening symptoms but can be very painful.

Venom
A predominantly neurotoxic venom that may affect breathing. Bites can be very painful with some swelling. There is no antivenom for the bite of this snake.

The Cape Coral Snake has an orange head.

 FIRST AID

- Immobilise and reassure the victim, who must lie down and remain as still as possible.
- Immediately arrange transport to a hospital.
- Resort to artificial respiration if necessary.

KUNENE CORAL SNAKE

Aspidelaps lubricus cowlesi

VERY DANGEROUS

Average length
50cm

Maximum length
80cm

Distribution

Found in central and northern Namibia into southern Angola. Widespread but not often seen, as it largely lives underground, emerging at night, often after decent rains.

Colour

Grey to brown body, often with hints of orange and yellow. There are dark crossbars on the body that range from distinct to barely visible. The head is darker above, being black to dark brown. The underside is white to cream with distinct dark bars on the throat.

Preferred habitat

Usually found in rocky, dry regions across Namibia. May be found under rocks, but appears to spend much of its time underground.

Habits

Spends much of its time underground, but is known to be active at night, especially after decent rain. It will forage for food at night and has been documented entering houses, where most bites have taken place.

AT A GLANCE

- Grey to brown body, often with hints of orange and with faint darker bands
- Snout has a distinct large rostral scale
- Mostly moves around at night
- Usually found around rocky outcrops in dry regions

The bars on the body fade with age.

Luke Kemp

72

This snake will lift its head well off the ground and form a hood when threatened.

Note the large rostral scale, which the snake uses for burrowing.

Individuals in southern Angola may not have dark bars on the body or a dark head.

Similar species
Its colour and shape make it quite distinct and easy to identify. It is occasionally mistaken for an eel.

Enemies
Other snakes and small carnivores. They are also frequently hit by vehicles at night whilst crossing roads.

Food
Probably lizards, snakes, small rodents and frogs.

Reproduction
Lays between 3–11 eggs in summer. The hatchlings measure about 17–18cm.

Danger to humans
This species has recently accounted for four human fatalities – mostly children.

Venom
Not much is known about the venom. It appears to be neurotoxic and potentially lethal. It remains uncertain how effective antivenom is for bites from this snake. First-aiders may need to help the victim breathe.

FIRST AID

- Immobilise and reassure the victim, who must lie down and remain as still as possible.
- Immediately arrange transport to a hospital.
- Resort to artificial respiration if necessary.

Other names:
Shield-nose Cobra,
Skildneuskobra,
Skildneusslang

SPECKLED SHIELD-NOSE SNAKE

Aspidelaps scutatus scutatus

Distribution

The Speckled Shield-nose Snake occurs from just north of Pretoria in Gauteng, extending to western Mpumalanga, Limpopo, the northern North West Province and the Northern Cape, as well as to southern and western Zimbabwe, much of Botswana, excluding the southwest, and northern Namibia.

Colour

The Speckled Shield-nose Snake is pale grey-brown to salmon pink or reddish brown above with a series of liver blotches on the back and tail. The head and neck are largely black in adults with white markings on the throat region.

Preferred habitat

This snake inhabits sandy and stony regions in dry savannas.

Habits

The Speckled Shield-nose Snake hides during the day and forages at night; it is often seen after heavy rains. It has a very large scale on its nose, which it uses to bulldoze through soft sand. This snake is known to play dead, like the Rinkhals. If cornered, it will lift its head off the ground and strike repeatedly while hissing.

Average length
40–45cm

Maximum length
65cm

AT A GLANCE

- A short, thick snake
- Broad head with very large rostral scale
- Broad black band on the throat
- Lifts its head off the ground if threatened, but does not spread a hood
- Feigns death
- Active at night

The head and neck are largely black in colour.

The large shield on the nose is used to bulldoze through soft sand.

Similar species
May be confused with the tiger snakes and the Zebra Cobra, but can be distinguished by its short, stout body and the unique enlarged scale on the nose.

Enemies
Other snakes. Also popular in the pet trade.

Food
Snakes, frogs and small mammals. It also eats lizards, particularly legless lizards that live in loose sand.

Reproduction
Oviparous, lays 4–14 eggs in summer. Females have been observed coiling around their eggs. The young measure 16–18cm in length.

Danger to humans
Bites seldom result in life-threatening symptoms, but there has been one report of human death in a young child in Limpopo.

Venom
Mildly cytotoxic and neurotoxic, causing local swelling and necrosis. Ptosis (drooping eyelids) and blurred vision as well as paralysed facial muscles have also been reported. Respiratory failure may occur, but is rare. There is no antivenom for the bite of this snake.

This snake lifts its head off the ground if threatened, but does not form a hood.

 FIRST AID
- Immobilise and reassure the victim, who must lie down and remain as still as possible.
- Immediately arrange transport to a hospital.

Other names:
Zambezi Garter Snake,
Zambesikousbandslang,
Boulenger se
Kousbandslang

Average length
60cm

Maximum length
77cm

AT A GLANCE

- Medium-sized snake with rounded snout
- Juveniles have 9–20 narrow white to pale yellow bands on the back and tail
- May coil up and hiss if confronted, but does not spread a hood
- A quiet, sluggish snake that is reluctant to bite

BOULENGER'S GARTER SNAKE

Elapsoidea boulengeri

DANGEROUS

Distribution
Boulenger's Garter Snake occurs from northern KwaZulu-Natal into eastern Mpumalanga, Limpopo and into southern Mozambique, Zimbabwe and eastern Botswana.

Colour
Dark chocolate brown to black above, with narrow white bands on the body and tail, which usually fade with age. Juveniles have a white head, black back with 9–20 white to pale yellow bands on the body and tail. The belly is usually dark grey to brown but may occasionally be white.

Preferred habitat
This snake inhabits lowland forest and moist savanna, grassland and dry savanna.

Habits
Boulenger's Garter Snake is a nocturnal snake that largely lives underground and is seldom encountered. It is occasionally found at night on the move, especially after rain, or may be found under logs and rocks.

Similar species
May be confused with other Garter Snakes.

This snake's belly is usually dark but may occasionally be white.

Subadults may retain faint white bands that fade with age.

Enemies
Other snakes. Also killed by vehicles when crossing roads at night.

Food
Small reptiles, especially snakes, and frogs.

Reproduction
Oviparous, lays 4–10 eggs in summer. The young measure 15–17cm in length.

Danger to humans
Bites are not life-threatening, but a large individual can deliver a rather unpleasant bite.

Juveniles have a white to grey head with a black streak down the back of the head.

Venom
A relatively mildly cytotoxic and neurotoxic venom, causing immediate pain and stiffness in the affected limb. Nausea, disorientation and blurred vision may also be experienced. There is no antivenom for the bite of this snake and symptoms usually subside within a day.

Juveniles have 9–20 prominent pale bands.

 FIRST AID

- If you are sure that a Boulenger's Garter Snake was responsible for the bite, get the victim to a doctor, where the bite must be treated symptomatically.
- Painkillers may be required. Polyvalent antivenom is not effective.

BACK-FANGED SNAKES

Back-fanged snakes are common throughout southern Africa. Some species are particularly abundant and often encountered, such as the Herald Snake and the Short-snouted Grass Snake.

- Usually long and slender.
- Have small fangs on the upper jaw that are situated roughly below or behind the eyes. These fangs are not hollow; instead, they have a groove down the front, along which the venom will run for envenomation to occur.
- Most back-fanged snakes have mild venom, which has little or no effect on humans and domestic pets.
- Known fatalities caused only by Boomslangs and Vine Snakes. Both possess a potent haemotoxic venom.
- Mostly egg-laying.

Herald Snake

Spotted Skaapsteker

Boomslang

Vine Snake

Tiger Snake

Bibron's Stiletto Snake

Average length
1.2–1.5m

Maximum length
2.1m

AT A GLANCE

- A short, stubby head with enormous eyes
- Strongly keeled body scales
- May inflate the neck and most of the body if provoked
- Spends most of its life in trees
- Birds often signal its presence, especially bulbuls
- Active during the day

BOOMSLANG

Dispholidus typus

VERY DANGEROUS

Note: Some sources mention two subspecies of Boomslang in Southern Africa – the Cape Boomslang (*Dispholidus typus typus*) and the Common Boomslang (*Dispholidus typus viridis*). This needs further investigation and will be treated as a single species in this book.

Distribution

the Boomslang occurs from near Lambert's Bay in the Western Cape and extends southwards, as well as eastwards into the Eastern Cape, along the Wild Coast, and northwards into much of KwaZulu-Natal, Mpumalanga, northern Gauteng, Limpopo, parts of the North West Province, the northeastern Northern Cape and just entering the Free State. Also found in Eswatini, Mozambique, most of Zimbabwe, Botswana, and northern Namibia, as well as further north.

Colour

Juveniles are light grey to brown above with a darker band down the back and with a fine stippling of blue and orange/yellow on the neck that becomes prominent when the snake is threatened and inflates its body. The head is brown to grey above with clean

Male Boomslangs in northern regions are typically bright green.

79

Males in the Cape are generally black and yellow.

white lower jaw and upper lip. The enormous eyes are a brilliant emerald green. When the snake reaches a length of close to 1m, the colours change to those of the adult phase.

Most females are light to olive-brown or grey-brown with a dirty white to brown belly; some females may be green. Male Boomslang from the southwestern parts of the range are dark brown to black with a bright yellow to orange or brick red belly. Some individuals may be black with dark grey belly scales. Males in the northern populations are bright green above and below, with or without black-edged scales, which can give a crossbarred appearance. There are also further variations of these colours. From Durban to Gqeberha (Port Elizabeth) we see a slow transition in colours, with males becoming green with more black and slowly turning more yellow with black the further west one goes.

Preferred habitat
Found in a variety of habitats including Karoo scrub, arid and moist savanna, lowland forest, grassland and fynbos. Quite often encountered in areas with low shrubs and few trees. Frequents well-vegetated gardens, parks and other urban areas.

Habits
A mellow, shy snake that spends most of its time in trees and shrubs, but may descend to the ground to bask or hunt. It is quick to disappear up into the closest tree or shrub when disturbed, where it will be well camouflaged and difficult to spot. Hunting mostly takes place in trees and shrubs, but this snake will descend to the ground to feed and may be seen chasing chameleons and frogs. It will usually bite the chameleon, release it and bite again from another angle; this ensures envenomation, as the venom delivery system in back-fanged snakes is quite primitive. The Boomslang has good vision and has no difficulty in locating prey. Quite often the snake will freeze with its head cocked and lateral waves will sweep down the neck.

If provoked, the Boomslang may inflate its neck to more than double its normal size, as a warning. Eventually the snake may inflate its entire body and will strike sideways and forwards in a jerky motion. It is a popular fallacy that the Boomslang drops from trees to attack people and, because it is back-fanged, can only bite a small finger. This is untrue and the snake can open its mouth 170 degrees and easily bite an arm or leg.

Similar species
Often confused with the Black Mamba and the Green Mamba, the harmless green bush snakes and some of the sand snakes.

Females are typically grey to brown.

Note the rounded head and large eyes.

A female Boomslang inflating her neck

Enemies

Birds of prey and other snakes. Several birds, especially the bulbuls, harass this snake and may even attack it. The Grey-headed Bush Shrike sometimes attacks the Boomslang continually until it has been killed.

Food

Actively hunts chameleons and frogs, including the African Bullfrog, as well as other tree-living lizards, birds and their eggs, which are swallowed whole. Well known for raiding Sociable Weaver nests in parts of the Kalahari. Rodents are infrequently taken.

Reproduction

Oviparous, lays 8–14 eggs, but as many as 27, in late spring or early summer. The eggs are 27–53 × 18–37mm in size and are laid in hollow tree trunks, rotting logs or among leaf litter. The young measure 29–38cm in length.

Danger to humans

Drop for drop the Boomslang has the most potent venom in Africa, but is shy and very seldom bites. Most victims accidentally

Juvenile Boomslang showing the emerald green eye

The Boomslang has good vision, enabling it to spot prey or potential threats at a distance.

step on a basking Boomslang or are snake handlers. There is virtually no chance of being bitten simply by walking past a tree with a Boomslang.

Venom

The venom is potently haemotoxic, causing severe bleeding from mucous membranes, as well as internal bleeding. It can result in fatal haemorrhage if untreated. Although the venom is extremely potent, it is slow-acting and may take five to more than 30 hours to produce serious symptoms; however, fatalities among children have been reported in under 12 hours. An effective monovalent antivenom is available from South African Vaccine Producers. Suspected Boomslang bite victims should be hospitalised for at least 48 hours.

 FIRST AID

- Immobilise and reassure the victim, who must lie down and be kept as still as possible.
- Transport the victim to hospital.

SOUTHERN VINE SNAKE

Thelotornis capensis

Other names:
Twig Snake, Bird Snake, Takslang, Voëlslang

Average length
1m

Maximum length
1.47m

AT A GLANCE

- A perfectly camouflaged snake that resembles a twig
- A spear-shaped head and keyhole-shaped pupils
- A bright red-and-black tongue, which often flickers slowly
- Usually found in trees and shrubs quite close to the ground

---

VERY DANGEROUS

Other species
Eastern Vine Snake *Thelotornis mossambicanus*

Subspecies
Southern Vine Snake *Thelotornis capensis capensis*
Oates' Vine Snake *Thelotornis capensis oatesii*

Distribution
The Southern Vine Snake occurs from the extreme eastern parts of the Eastern Cape, northwards along the coast into coastal KwaZulu-Natal, Mpumalanga, northern Gauteng, Limpopo and the eastern North West Province, as well as Eswatini, southern Mozambique, southern Zimbabwe and eastern Botswana.

The Eastern Vine Snake occurs in central Mozambique and eastern Zimbabwe.

Oates' Vine Snake occurs from northern Mozambique, across northern and central Zimbabwe, into northern Botswana and across the Caprivi into northern Namibia.

Colour
The Vine Snakes are incredibly well camouflaged and, when stationary, are extremely difficult to spot, as they resemble branches or vines. They are ash grey to grey-brown above with

Southern Vine Snakes are amazingly well camouflaged and resemble branches or vines.

black, orange and pink flecks and blotches. There are usually one or two dark blotches on the sides of the neck. The top of the head is usually pale blue to green and heavily speckled with dark brown, black and pink. A wide, pinkish-white, black-speckled band runs along the upper lip, from the snout to the back of the head, passing through the lower half of the eye. A dark oblique band radiates from each eye, down to the upper lip. The chin and throat are white with black speckles. The tongue is bright yellow to orange, or even red, and black-tipped.

Preferred habitat
This snake lives in trees and shrubs in lowland forest and moist and arid savanna.

Habits
A slender, mostly tree-living snake that prefers low shrubs, bushes, trees and hedges, where its cryptic coloration blends so well with its background that it is seldom seen. It moves gracefully and swiftly when disturbed.

A timid and retiring snake, but, when threatened, it will inflate its neck to display the pale skin between the scales, and its bright tongue will flicker in a wavy motion. Once the neck is inflated, it will not hesitate to strike and lunges to do so.

It actively hunts for food during the day, first approaching in short spurts, then darting forward to seize its prey; while doing so, its head may quiver, like a leaf in the wind. The prey is held firmly in the jaws while the venom takes effect. Generally more of an ambush hunter and remains very still in

When threatened, the Southern Vine Snake inflates its neck in self-defence.

This snake has keyhole-shaped pupils.

vegetation close to the ground, where it is extremely well camouflaged and has a good view of potential prey passing below; it will then descend quickly to the ground to catch it. Like the Boomslang, it will chew on its prey in order for envenomation to be effective. It may then take its prey into a tree or shrub and swallow it head first while hanging down.

Similar species
The Vine Snake may be confused with some of the sand snakes or grass snakes, but is usually found in trees and shrubs and can be differentiated by its rather unique and cryptic coloration. May also be confused with

The head is spear-shaped.

juvenile Boomslang but has a more slender, pointed head.

Enemies

Birds of prey and other snakes. Birds will often signal the presence of this snake by giving off distress calls and mobbing the snake; since it is relatively slow-moving, it is then easily killed. Also frequently killed by passing vehicles while crossing roads.

Food

Feeds largely on chameleons and frogs, including rain frogs, snakes and lizards. It is particularly fond of the harmless green bush snakes and the Green Water Snake. Birds are seldom taken, although fledglings and eggs provide an easy meal. Some small mammals, including bats, are also taken. This snake usually swallows its prey while hanging down from a branch.

Reproduction

Oviparous, lays 4–18 eggs in summer, which are 25–41 × 12–17mm. The young measure 25cm in length. May produce more than one clutch in a season and the eggs can take up to three months to hatch. Males are known

The tongue is bright red with a black tip.

The snake is difficult to detect among branches.

to engage in combat and will intertwine their bodies, while attempting to push their opponent's head down.

Danger to humans

The Vine Snake is very shy and placid, much like the Boomslang, and will only bite when severely provoked, i.e. when captured or stood on. Bites are extremely rare.

Venom

The venom of the Vine Snake is dangerously haemotoxic and has a similar effect to that of the Boomslang, causing bleeding from the mucous membranes, as well as internal bleeding. There is no antivenom, but human fatalities are unknown in southern Africa. Other species of Vine Snakes in central Africa have accounted for human fatalities.

 FIRST AID

- Immobilise and reassure the victim, who must lie down and be kept as still as possible.
- Transport the victim to hospital.

BIBRON'S STILETTO SNAKE

Atractaspis bibronii

DANGEROUS

Average length
30cm

Maximum length
70cm

Distribution

Occurs from southern KwaZulu-Natal into Mpumalanga, the Free State, the northern and eastern Northern Cape, Gauteng, Limpopo and the North West Province, as well as Eswatini, Mozambique, most of Zimbabwe, Botswana and northern Namibia, with random individuals found in the rest of the Northern Cape and southern Namibia.

Colour

Uniform purple-brown to light brown, dark brown or blackish above, except prior to shedding when the snake has a bluish-grey appearance. The belly is similar in colour to the back, but in some areas, especially in the north, the belly will be white to creamy.

Preferred habitat

This snake is found in a wide variety of habitats including lowland forest, moist and arid savanna, Karoo scrub, grassland and desert.

Habits

This burrowing snake is often found under logs or rocks and in deserted termite mounds, particularly by youngsters looking

AT A GLANCE

- A fairly inconspicuous snake with small eyes, often presumed harmless
- Uniform purple-brown to dark brown or blackish
- Neck may arch just behind the head
- Tail ends in a sharp spine
- Often found under logs or rocks
- Active on warm, wet summer nights

Bibron's Stiletto Snakes are nondescript and are easily mistaken for harmless snakes. They are often picked up by people, resulting in bites.

for snakes. It emerges on warm and wet summer nights, especially after heavy rains. Often exposed during earth-moving works or excavations.

An irascible snake that bites readily. The head is small and rounded and the large fangs positioned horizontally, pointing towards the back of the jaw; the fangs are slightly moveable, enabling the snake to extend a fang on either side of the upper jaw, even when the mouth is closed. It has a small gape and cannot bite in the same way as most venomous snakes. It is impossible to hold this snake safely behind the head, as it merely twists the head sideways to pierce a finger. It may also press the hard, sharp tip of its tail against the person holding it, giving the impression that it is biting. To envenomate its prey in underground burrows, it will extend a fang, move its head over its prey and press downwards in a stabbing fashion.

Similar species

This dangerous little snake is easily confused with a variety of other inconspicuous snakes, such as the purple-glossed snakes, the Natal Black Snake, the wolf snakes and the Black File Snake. It is often confused with the harmless Mole Snake and picked up, even though it does not resemble a juvenile Mole Snake.

Enemies

Birds of prey and small mammalian carnivores, as well as other snakes.

Food

A variety of burrowing reptiles such as small snakes and especially sleeping lizards and their eggs, as well as frogs and small rodents, especially nestlings.

Reproduction

Oviparous, lays 3–7 eggs in midsummer, which are 27–36 × 10–12mm. The young measure 15cm in length.

Danger to humans

Although no fatalities have been recorded in southern Africa, this snake delivers an extremely painful bite, and envenomation often leads to the loss of a finger. Bites are

Specimens in the northern parts of the region may have white bellies that extend up the sides of the body.

These snakes will often arch the neck when exposed and move with erratic twitchy movements.

common in KwaZulu-Natal, Mpumalanga, Limpopo, Eswatini and Mozambique. Snake enthusiasts and game rangers are often bitten, generally mistaking this snake for something harmless, like a Wolf Snake. It usually bites the moment it is handled, and victims often suffer several bites before dropping the snake.

Venom

The venom is predominantly cytotoxic, causing painful swelling that may result in necrosis. In some instances, mild neurotoxic symptoms such as nausea and a dry throat can occur. The site around the bite usually turns blue, and blistering may follow. Other symptoms can include headaches, difficulty in swallowing and painful eye movements. There is no antivenom for the bite of this snake. If bitten on the hand, it should be moved continuously for 10–20 minutes and massaged to spread the venom and reduce the chance of local tissue damage. Bites must be treated symptomatically and treatment will consist largely of rehydration and administering painkillers. Large blisters can be drained, but it is not advisable to cut at the site of the bite within the first six or seven days, as this may result in secondary infection.

The fangs are moveable and can protrude sideways from of the mouth.

The large, horizontal fangs of Bibron's Stiletto Snake point towards the back of the jaw.

 FIRST AID

- Elevate the affected limb.
- Transport the victim to hospital.

Average length
60–90cm

Maximum length
1.2m

AT A GLANCE

- A stout snake with a small, blunt head
- Small eyes with round pupils
- Usually uniform inky or jet black
- Moves slowly and deliberately
- Usually found in leaf litter or damp, forested areas
- May be seen crossing roads after heavy rains
- Sometimes falls into swimming pools

NATAL BLACK SNAKE
Macrelaps microlepidotus

DANGEROUS

Distribution
Endemic to South Africa, occurs in the Eastern Cape, extending northwards to KwaZulu-Natal. Occurs from sea level to about 1,300m at Nkandla and Estcourt.

Colour
Usually a uniform inky or jet black above and below with pale skin visible between the scales. Becomes a dull grey colour prior to shedding.

Preferred habitat
Damp localities in lowland forest and along streams in coastal bush. Also found in suburban gardens. Especially common around Stutterheim in the Eastern Cape and Hilton and Kloof in KwaZulu-Natal.

Habits
A docile snake that is very reluctant to bite. Usually found under rotting logs or stones, in leaf litter, animal burrows and storm water drains. May be seen moving about slowly and deliberately on warm, overcast days or warm, damp nights. It is a good swimmer and has been observed swimming in forest streams. Lives largely underground, where it searches for food. It usually grabs its prey, wraps a few coils around it and then chews it to enable the venom to penetrate.

This snake has white skin between the scales.

The Natal Black Snake lives mostly underground and is fond of burrowing.

Similar species

May be confused with Bibron's Stiletto Snake, the Wolf Snake or any of the purple-glossed snakes or dark Mole Snakes.

Enemies

Other snakes and birds of prey, as well as small mammalian carnivores.

Food

Frogs, especially rain frogs, legless lizards, snakes and small rodents. Also known to feed on carrion.

Prior to shedding, these snakes turn grey.

It has tiny eyes.

The tongue is pink with white tips.

Reproduction

Oviparous, lays 3–10 eggs in summer, which are 38–56 × 23–31mm. The young measure 20–29cm in length.

Danger to humans

The venom of this snake has not been studied and bites are extremely rare.

Venom

This snake very rarely features in snakebite accidents, but one recorded bite apparently resulted in loss of consciousness for approximately 30 minutes. Antivenom is not effective against the venom of this snake and should not be used.

FIRST AID

• **Transport the victim to hospital.**

OLIVE GRASS SNAKE

Psammophis mossambicus

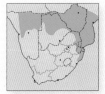

MILDLY VENOMOUS

Distribution
KwaZulu-Natal, from just north of Durban, northwards into Mpumalanga and Limpopo, as well as Mozambique, Eswatini, Zimbabwe, northern Botswana and northern Namibia.

Colour
Uniform olive-brown to yellowish above or with black-edged scales on the back that may form dark longitudinal lines, often with scattered black scales on the neck and chin. The lips are pale with finely black-edged brown spots or blotches on the upper lip. The underside is white to yellowish, sometimes with darker spots and mottling.

Preferred habitat
Moist savanna and lowland forest. Often found close to water.

Habits
A robust, active and fast-moving diurnal snake that hastens for cover when disturbed. It is nervous and will remain hidden unless flushed out. Like the Black Mamba, it lifts up to a third of its body well off the ground, especially when on the move.

Although mainly ground-living, it climbs onto shrubs and bushes to bask. Many individuals have truncated tails – the result of injuries sustained during encounters with predators. This snake can often be seen crossing roads in lowveld and low-lying areas and moves very quickly when doing so.

Average length
1m

Maximum length
1.8m

AT A GLANCE

- A fairly large, robust and very fast-moving snake
- Elongate body with long thin tail
- May have faint patterning on the head, especially in juveniles
- May have dark speckling on the upper lip
- Eyes have round pupils
- Bites readily if captured
- Very active during the day
- May move with the head held off the ground, similar to a Black Mamba or Boomslang

This snake is easily mistaken for a female Boomslang or Black Mamba.

Luke Kemp

90

Diurnal, the Olive Grass Snake may be seen basking in the morning sun.

Similar species

Often mistaken for the Black Mamba, the Boomslang and some of the other sand snakes and grass snakes, especially the Short-snouted Grass Snake.

Enemies

Other snakes, birds of prey and small carnivores, such as mongooses. Often killed by vehicles while crossing roads.

Food

Lizards, small mammals, frogs and other snakes, including the Black Mamba and the Puff Adder. Small birds are also taken. Adults feed on much larger rodents than other grass snakes.

Reproduction

Oviparous, lays 10–30 eggs in midsummer, which are 28–40 × 10–20mm. The young average 27–30cm in length.

Danger to humans

This snake does not pose any danger to humans, although large specimens can deliver a painful bite.

Venom

A mild venom that may cause local pain, a little swelling and occasionally nausea.

Juveniles are usually well patterned.

Females lay from 10–30 eggs.

 FIRST AID

- Take the victim to a doctor or hospital for the bite to be treated symptomatically.

Other names:
Short-snouted
Whip Snake, Short-
snouted Sand Snake,
Kortsnoetgrasslang,
Kortsnoetsweepslang

SHORT-SNOUTED GRASS SNAKE

Psammophis brevirostris

MILDLY VENOMOUS

Average length
60cm

Maximum length
1.2m

AT A GLANCE

- An active, alert and fast-moving snake
- Dark brown or black stripes down the body
- Plain forms are also known
- Quite large eyes with round pupils
- Easily confused with the larger Olive Grass Snake
- Quickly dashes for cover when disturbed
- Bites readily when handled
- Largely found at higher elevation grassland and bushveld

Distribution

Occurs from the Eastern Cape northwards into most of KwaZulu-Natal, Mpumalanga, Gauteng, the North West Province, the northeastern Northern Cape and Limpopo, as well as Eswatini, parts of Mozambique, eastern Zimbabwe, southern Botswana and central Namibia.

Colour

Olive-brown above with a pale, dashed median line, flanked on either side by up to three rows of dark brown or black-edged scales, which may form narrow stripes. A narrow, lighter brown line borders the black lines dorsolaterally. The sides are usually light brown to red-brown. Plain forms are occasionally seen. The underside is white or yellowish, sometimes with a line of black spots on each side.

Preferred habitat

Grassland, moist savanna and lowland forest in the east, and Karoo scrub and desert in the west.

The Short-snouted Grass Snake lays from 4–15 eggs in summer.

A dashed median line, flanked by brown scales, is common in this snake.

Habits

An alert, fast-moving snake that dashes for cover when disturbed and will remain motionless until flushed out. It may venture onto low shrubs to bask. Like the Olive Grass Snake, it is quick to bite if handled. If captured by its tail, the Short-snouted Grass Snake will vigorously spin around and this may result in the tip of the tail breaking off and the snake escaping. This is an active diurnal hunter that chases after fast-moving prey, such as lizards.

Similar species

Easily confused with other sand snakes and grass snakes, especially the Olive Grass Snake. Can also be mistaken for a small Black Mamba.

Enemies

Other snakes, small mammals and birds of prey.

Food

Snakes, rodents, small birds and lizards, especially skinks.

Reproduction

Oviparous, this snake lays 4–15 eggs in summer, eggs measuring 23–40 × 10–20mm. The young measure 19–27cm in length. Females may produce more than one clutch per season.

Danger to humans

None.

Venom

Not thought to be harmful.

The underside of its body is often yellowish.

Average length
70cm–1m

Maximum length
1.4m

AT A GLANCE

- A long, slender, striped snake
- A pointed head
- Large eyes with round pupils
- Lemon yellow belly
- Usually has spots or barring on the neck
- Very fast-moving
- Active during the day
- May climb bushes and shrubs
- Common around houses and lodges

WESTERN YELLOW-BELLIED SAND SNAKE

Psammophis subtaeniatus

MILDLY VENOMOUS

Distribution
Occurs from northern KwaZulu-Natal northwards into Mpumalanga, Gauteng, the North West Province and Limpopo, as well as Eswatini, eastern Mozambique, Zimbabwe, eastern and northern Botswana, northern Namibia and into Angola and Zambia.

Colour
Greyish brown to olive-grey or dark brown above with a broad, black-edged brown band running down the back; this is bordered by a narrow cream to yellow stripe on either side, then a dark brown lateral band with a black line on the lower edge. The head has pale markings, edged with dark brown, which form transverse bars onto the neck. The middle of the belly is bright lemon yellow, bordered on either side by a black hairline stripe; the outer portions of the belly are pure white. Individuals from northern Botswana are often plain forms without the above patterns.

Preferred habitat
Arid savanna, especially mopane veld and acacia veld. Very common in the Zambezi and Limpopo valleys.

Luke Kemp

When disturbed, this fast-moving snake is quick to escape.

Habits

This is one of South Africa's fastest snakes. It is common throughout most of its range. Like most of the grass and sand snakes, it is active during the day, often in the hottest hours. It moves off quickly if disturbed, only to freeze when it gets to the nearest bush or shrub. It relies on its excellent camouflage to escape detection. Though ground-dwelling, it may bask or seek food in shrubs and low bushes. If captured by its tail, it will vigorously spin around and this may result in the tip of the tail breaking off and the snake escaping; the broken tail will twitch, drawing the attention of predators.

It has transverse bars on the side of its head.

In the northern parts of their range they may be darker brown or even plain brown to grey.

This snake coils around its prey to secure it.

Although terrestrial, this snake may climb to bask.

Similar species

Easily confused with the other sand and grass snakes and the equally harmless Striped Skaapsteker.

Enemies

Other snakes and birds of prey.

Food

Prefers lizards, but also eats frogs, rodents and small birds.

Reproduction

Oviparous, lays 4–10 eggs in summer, which are 32 × 12mm. The young measure 20cm in length.

Danger to humans

None.

Venom

Not thought to be harmful.

SPOTTED SKAAPSTEKER

Psammophylax rhombeatus

MILDLY VENOMOUS

Distribution

Most of South Africa, excluding the central Northern Cape, the northwestern Free State and most of the North West Province. Also extends into Namibia.

Colour

There are two common colour variations: in KwaZulu-Natal, this snake is pale brown to yellow-brown or dark brown above, with two yellowish stripes down the body, and dark-edged brown scales near the belly that form dark lines; alternatively, there may be dark blotches down the sides; the head is dark brownish with a lighter upper lip. Elsewhere in southern Africa, this snake is light silvery-grey above with black-edged darker blotches on the back and sides; the dark blotches on the back can form a pattern; it may have orange dots and speckles; the head is dark brownish with a white upper lip and a dark patch behind the eye; the underside is usually white to yellowish with spots and blotches and may be quite colourful.

Average length 45–85cm

Maximum length
May exceed 1.4m

Preferred habitat

Found from the coast to mountaintops, where it inhabits fynbos, grassland, moist savanna and semi-desert areas.

AT A GLANCE

- Fairly large eyes with round pupils
- Long slender tail
- Top of the head is plain brown to grey
- Usually with paired spots down the back
- May be striped in KwaZulu-Natal and the Free State
- Nervous and fast-moving
- Dashes for cover when disturbed
- Shelters under rocks and logs
- Active during the day

Luke Kemp

The Spotted Skaapsteker favours grasslands or fynbos habitat.

Habits

An alert, fast-moving, diurnal snake that actively hunts its prey. It is nervous and very quick to disappear into grass or shrubs when disturbed; it will freeze and may even coil around a grass tuft and is well camouflaged. It also shelters under rocks and logs. Like the Rinkhals, it is known to play dead when threatened.

The name 'skaapsteker', which translates to 'sheep stabber', originated with the sheep farmers who lost their sheep to snakebite. They mistakenly blamed the more common Spotted Skaapsteker, instead of the Cape Cobra, which was most likely responsible.

Similar species

May be confused with the sand snakes and other grass snakes as well as juvenile Mole Snakes and the Dwarf Beaked Snake.

Enemies

Birds of prey and small mammalian carnivores, as well as other snakes.

Food

Feeds mostly on rodents, lizards, birds, frogs and other snakes. Has been observed anchoring its tail and digging for rain frogs in soft sand, using its head as a shovel.

This snake actively hunts its prey.

Ashley Kemp

The eyes are typically red with a black pupil.

Reproduction

Oviparous, lays 8–30 eggs in summer, which are 20–35 × 12–18mm. Females usually lay their eggs under rocks and will coil around them during incubation. Multiple females may use the same rock and have a communal nesting site. The embryos are partially developed when the eggs are laid and this results in a reduced incubation period of about six weeks. The young measure 15.5–24cm in length.

Danger to humans

The venom is mild and of no consequence to humans.

Venom

Not thought to be harmful. May cause some swelling and slight discoloration if the snake is allowed to chew.

An individual from KwaZulu-Natal with two characteristic yellowish stripes running down its body.

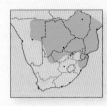

EASTERN TIGER SNAKE

Telescopus semiannulatus

MILDLY VENOMOUS

Average length
50–80cm

Maximum length
1m

AT A GLANCE

- Head is distinct from the slender body
- 22–75 dark brown to blackish crossbars or blotches on the body and tail
- Large eyes with vertical pupils
- Lifts its head and strikes viciously when threatened
- Often found crossing tarred roads after heavy rains
- Active at night

Note: There are two similar-looking tiger snakes: Beetz's Tiger Snake, which occurs from the Western Cape to the Northern Cape and into Namibia; and the Western Tiger Snake, which ranges from the northern part of the Northern Cape to Namibia.

Distribution
From central KwaZulu-Natal extending into Mpumalanga, Gauteng, Limpopo, the North West Province and the Northern Cape, as well as Mozambique, Eswatini, Zimbabwe, Botswana and northern Namibia.

Colour
Orange-pink to dull salmon pink or orange-brown above with 22–75 dark brown to blackish crossbars or saddle-like blotches on the body and tail. The underside is yellowish to orange-pink.

Preferred habitat
Found in a variety of habitats, largely in rocky regions of desert, Karoo scrub, arid and moist savanna and lowland forest.

Habits
A nocturnal, slow-moving snake that spends most of its day concealed under loose flakes of rock, in rock crevices or under tree bark. Though largely a ground-dweller, it often ventures into trees, shrubs and old buildings, where it hunts for food. After

This snake puts up an impressive display if threatened.

summer rains, it often crosses tarred roads and many are killed by passing vehicles. Like the Herald Snake, it puts on an impressive display when threatened or cornered, raising its head off the ground with the lips flared out to the side and striking with intent.

Similar species

Due to the dark, saddle-like blotches on the back, it may be confused with the coral snakes, the shield-nose snakes or the Zebra Cobra in Namibia.

Enemies

Small mammalian carnivores and other snakes.

Food

Mainly feeds on lizards, especially geckos. Fledgling birds, bats and small rodents are also eaten.

Reproduction

Oviparous, lays 3–20 eggs in summer, which are 24–55 × 10–17mm. The young measure 17–23cm in length.

Eastern Tiger Snake feeding on a Dwarf Gecko

The head is distinct from the body, and the large eyes have vertical pupils.

Danger to humans

None.

Venom

Not thought to be harmful to humans.

Tiger Snakes are adept climbers, often scaling trees or rafters in search of geckos and bats.

HERALD SNAKE
Crotaphopeltis hotamboeia

MILDLY VENOMOUS

Average length 30–70cm

**Maximum length
1m**

Distribution
Extends from the Western Cape and just entering the Northern Cape, across the Eastern Cape into KwaZulu-Natal, Mpumalanga, Gauteng, Limpopo, the North West Province and the Free State, as well as Lesotho, Eswatini, Mozambique, Zimbabwe, Botswana and further north.

Colour
Olive-green, light brown or grey above, sometimes with white speckles that may form transverse bars, especially in juveniles. The temporal region is glossy, iridescent black to blue-black and gives the head a much darker appearance than the body. The upper lip is bright red, orange-red, yellowish, white or blackish; the red lip colour is not commonly found in Zululand and Zimbabwe. The underside is mother-of-pearl cream. The young have distinctive dark heads.

Preferred habitat
Very common in marshy areas, fynbos, lowland forest, moist savanna and grassland.

AT A GLANCE

- Iridescent blue-black head, which is much darker than the rest of the body
- Upper lip may be bright red, orange-red, yellowish, white or blackish
- May have white speckles on the body
- Found in damp localities
- Common in suburban gardens
- Active at night

When threatened, the Herald Snake adopts a defensive posture with a raised, flattened head and flared lips.

The conspicuous orange-red upper lip is an identifying feature in parts of its range.

The head is darker than the rest of the body.

Habits
A common and widespread snake that prefers damp localities. Often found in suburban gardens, where it seeks shelter in rockeries, under building rubble, gate motors, electrical boxes and in compost heaps. Due to its nocturnal habits, it is sometimes incorrectly referred to as a night adder. When this snake grabs its prey in its jaws, it will hang onto it while its venom takes effect. When threatened, it will coil back, raise its head well off the ground and flatten it horizontally, flaring the lips and striking repeatedly. The Herald Snake and Brown House Snake are by far the most commonly encountered snakes in South African gardens.

Similar species
Not easily confused with other snakes, but due to its nocturnal habits, it is sometimes called a night adder, although there is no real resemblance.

Enemies
Small mammalian carnivores, birds and other snakes. The young can be killed by spiders.

Food
Feeds on amphibians, including the rain frog, and has a preference for toads. The occasional lizard is also eaten. In captivity, it is also known to eat other snakes.

Reproduction
Oviparous, lays 6–19 eggs in early summer, which are 25–32 × 10–13mm. The young measure 8–18cm in length. Females may produce more than one clutch per season.

Danger to humans
None.

Venom
Not thought to be harmful.

It is one of the most commonly encountered snakes, often found in suburban gardens.

101

PAINFUL BITES

Two snakes in southern Africa, despite being non-venomous, can inflict a painful bite. The Southern African Python is widespread in the eastern and northern parts of southern Africa. The Mole Snake is widespread across much of Africa. Although both snakes are not aggressive, if cornered or an attempt is made to pick them up or catch them, both snakes can inflict a painful bite that often requires stitches and some medical attention. Historically, pythons in Africa have accounted for human fatalities, although these are rare in southern Africa.

- Pythons are easily identified by the large size and distinct pattern.
- Mole snakes vary in colour and may be confused with a number of venomous snakes, especially cobras. Mole Snakes are bulky with small, pointed heads.
- Pythons lay eggs, usually in an empty animal burrow. They are known to curl around the eggs until they hatch, around 90 days later.
- Mole Snakes give live birth and can drop from 25–50 young. The young are pale with dark spots that may form zigzag patterns down the back. These patterns will fade after the snake reaches around 60cm.

Mole Snake

Southern African Python

Southern African Python

Mole Snake

Mole Snake

SOUTHERN AFRICAN PYTHON

Python natalensis

DANGEROUS

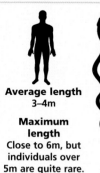

**Average length
3–4m**

**Maximum
length**
Close to 6m, but
individuals over
5m are quite rare.

Distribution

From the extreme northeastern coast of the Eastern Cape, extending through KwaZulu-Natal into Mpumalanga, Gauteng, Limpopo, the North West Province and just entering the Northern Cape and the Free State. Throughout Mozambique, Eswatini, Zimbabwe, eastern and northern Botswana and much of central and northern Namibia. There is also a relict population in the Eastern Cape near the Fish River Reserve, which was once believed to have been eliminated, but animals were reintroduced in the 1990s.

Colour

Dark brown above with grey-brown blotches, and dark speckling and widely spaced, dark brown blotches on the sides. There is a dark brown arrowhead marking on the crown of the head. There is often a pale stripe down the tail. The underside is white to dirty white with dark blotches. The young are usually quite light in colour with vivid markings. Breeding females with eggs are often very dark.

Preferred habitat

A widespread and common snake that is often found on rocky outcrops in arid and moist savanna, as well as lowland forest. Often associated with large animal burrows in flat areas, away from rocky outcrops. May also be found in swamps and reed beds. Comfortable in water, and younger snakes are often seen hunting birds in trees.

AT A GLANCE

- Southern Africa's largest and bulkiest snake
- Has heat sensory pits on the upper and lower lips
- Likes to bask in the sun, especially after a meal
- Partial to water and often dives into pools to escape
- Mainly active at dusk and at night

The underside is white to dirty white with dark blotches.

103

Heat pits are visible on the snout.

Habits

This snake is fond of basking, especially after a meal, but is more active at dusk and at night. It is fond of water and will quickly dive into water if disturbed and can remain underwater for long periods.

Like boas, anacondas, rattlesnakes and pit vipers, it has heat sensory pits on the jaws, which enable it to detect warm-blooded prey in pitch darkness. These heat sensors act as infrared vision and can detect differences in temperature.

It is an ambush hunter and may spend several weeks in one spot awaiting prey. It latches onto its prey with its powerful and strongly recurved teeth and then constricts it. Contrary to popular belief, this snake does not crush its prey to death and seldom breaks bones in the process; instead, it applies a great deal of pressure to the chest region and death results from circulatory arrest. It is also a misconception that the python needs to anchor its tail to a tree before it can constrict its prey.

This snake is of great value to farmers, as it helps to control cane rats and dassies. Unfortunately, it is still persecuted and killed when located. It is widely used in local traditional medicine and has been listed as a protected species in most countries.

Similar species

This large, bulky snake is not easily confused with other snakes.

Enemies

Mongooses, meerkats, crocodiles, wild dogs, hyaenas, honey badgers, leopards and other snakes. Many are killed at night while crossing roads. Both the skin and fat are used in traditional medicine.

Food

Cane rats, dassies, hares, monkeys, small antelope and game birds, as well as fish, monitor lizards and crocodiles. Juveniles feed largely on rodents and birds. Domestic animals, especially dogs, are often eaten, as are farm animals.

A young Southern African Python in defensive mode, ready to strike.

This snake can strike to a distance of at least half the length of its body.

Pythons have over 80 long, recurved teeth, which are used like fishing hooks to secure prey.

Reproduction

Oviparous, lays 30–60 eggs in midsummer, depending on the size of the female, but can lay over 100 eggs. The eggs are 8–10 × 6–8cm – a little smaller than a tennis ball – and weigh 130–160g. Eggs are often laid in aardvark holes or hollowed out termite mounds; the female will coil around the eggs throughout the three-month incubation period. During this time, she will not feed, but may leave the eggs to bask or drink water. Basking will generate extra body heat – the body temperature may increase to 40°C; this will be transferred to the eggs when the female coils around them.

The young measure 50–70cm. If undisturbed, they will remain with the mother for two to three weeks before moving off on their own. They can take up to 10 years to reach sexual maturity.

Young pythons spend much of their lives in trees.

Danger to humans

Pythons have been known to kill people in the past, although rarely so; today's Southern African Python is smaller and exceptionally large individuals are rare. This snake does lunge and bite readily and, due to its size and array of strong, recurved teeth, a bite can result in considerable damage and the victim may require stitches. It is not a venomous snake

FIRST AID

- Bandage the wound to stop the bleeding.
- Transport promptly to hospital.

MOLE SNAKE

Pseudaspis cana

HARMLESS

Average length
80cm–1.4m

Maximum length
2.2m

AT A GLANCE

- A small head with a pointed snout
- Round pupils
- Varies in colour, but adults usually lack markings
- Light brown to reddish brown in Gauteng
- Spends most of its time underground
- Active during the day

Distribution

Found throughout most of southern Africa. Avoids thick forest and dry desert.

Colour

Adults are usually uniform light grey to light brown, dark brown, brick red or black above; the underside is yellowish, sometimes with darker patches. In Gauteng, this snake is usually light brown to reddish brown. Adults may retain some of the juvenile patterning. Juveniles are very different and are never plain in colour; they are light reddish brown to greyish brown with dark, usually zigzag markings, whitish spots and mottling above; white to yellowish below, sometimes with darker patches.

Preferred habitat

A variety of habitats, including mountainous regions and even coastal dunes. Particularly common in sandy, scrub-covered and grassveld regions.

Habits

A large, powerful constrictor with a small head and a pointed snout, which are very well adapted for a burrowing existence. It spends most of its time underground in search of food and is not commonly seen, other than in the Western Cape, Eastern Cape and parts of the Northern Cape. It navigates underground tunnels in search of mole-rats and other rodents. Its prey is usually seized by the head and constricted.

Golden-brown Mole Snake from Gauteng

Juveniles are patterned.

Adults are uniformly coloured.

Although this snake is not venomous, it can be quite vicious when threatened and will hiss and lunge forward with its mouth agape. Unfortunately, this snake is often mistaken for a Black Mamba or cobra and is killed on sight.

Similar species
May be confused with the Black Mamba or a cobra, especially the Cape Cobra. Young Mole Snakes are quite colourful and may be confused with the Dwarf Beaked Snake, Spotted Skaapsteker or Common Night Adder.

Enemies
Predatory birds, mammalian carnivores and other snakes, especially Cape Cobras. Many individuals are killed by vehicles while basking on or crossing roads.

Food
Adults feed on rats, mole-rats, gerbils and other small mammals. It also eats birds, as well as their eggs, which are swallowed whole. Juveniles feed largely on lizards and baby rodents.

This snake has a small head with a pointed snout.

Reproduction
Viviparous, gives birth to 25–50 young in late summer, although this can be as many as 95. The young measure 20–31cm in length. Adult males are known to engage in combat during the mating season, biting one another and inflicting nasty wounds, often exposing ribs and resulting in permanent scarring.

Danger to humans
Although not venomous, the Mole Snake has razor-sharp teeth and is capable of a painful bite. The snake performs a tin-opener action, causing the teeth to slice across the skin, making cuts which may require stitches.

FIRST AID

- If the bite pierces the skin, treat like any other cut or abrasion.
- Stitches may be required.

COMMON FANGLESS AND NON-VENOMOUS SNAKES

Fangless snakes do not possess venom but may have rows of small, sharp teeth used to grab prey. As these snakes do not have venom, they have adapted other feeding strategies to overpower their prey. Many species use constriction to kill their prey, but other species may swallow the prey live. They are widespread throughout southern Africa. Snakes like the Brown House Snake frequent human dwellings and are often encountered, but some fangless snakes, such as the Common File Snake, live in animal burrows and are quite rare in parts of their range.

- Vary in shape and size.
- Do not have fangs or venom glands but do have teeth.
- Mostly egg-laying, but there are exceptions, such as Common Slug-eater.

Spotted Bush Snake

Common Egg-eater

Brown House Snake

Green Water Snake

Brown Water Snake

Aurora House Snake

Luke Kemp

Luke Kemp

Average length 60–90cm

Maximum length
1.5m

AT A GLANCE

- A spear-shaped head distinct from a slender body; old specimens may be stout
- Two whitish stripes extending across the face
- Very common near houses
- Active at night
- May have pale mottles or stripes down the side of the neck

BROWN HOUSE SNAKE
Boaedon capensis

HARMLESS

A common and widespread species across much of southern Africa. The Brown House Snake frequents human dwellings and urban areas, where it hunts rodents, bats, lizards and birds. It is great at controlling rat and other rodent populations. Colour is uniform light brown to reddish brown, dark brown to olive-brown. A whitish stripe runs from the tip of the nose, across the upper part of the eye, to the back of the head; a second whitish stripe may extend below the eye to the back of the jaw. These stripes may extend down the side of the body, forming pale mottled patterns. The underside is yellowish to mother-of-pearl white. It is a nocturnal snake but may be found during the day sheltering under building rubble, logs or rocks and corrugated sheets. It is quick to bite if handled, but poses no threats to humans or pets. It is not easily confused with other snakes due to the distinct pale stripe above the eye.

A reddish-brown adult from KwaZulu-Natal

A white stripe runs from the tip of its nose to the back of its head.

Ashley Kemp

AURORA HOUSE SNAKE

Lamprophis aurora

HARMLESS

Average length
40–60cm

Maximum length
90cm

Widespread across southern and central South Africa and Lesotho. The Aurora House Snake favours damp areas in grassland, moist savanna and fynbos. It is occasionally found in human dwellings, especially in southern Johannesburg as well as around Cape Town. It hunts for nestling rodents, lizards and frogs, largely at night. Colour is olive to olive-brown or yellowish with a distinct spotted orange stripe down the centre of the back. The lower sides of the body may have a thin pale stripe blending into the white belly. Juveniles are often much darker than adults. It is a nocturnal snake but may be found during the day sheltering under building rubble, logs or rocks and garden pots or in compost heaps. It is incredibly docile and unlikely to bite, even if handled. The colours and pattern are quite distinctive to this species; however, it may be confused with the eastern form of the Spotted Harlequin.

This snake has a distinctive bright orange to yellow vertebral stripe.

AT A GLANCE

- Uniform olive-green to brown or yellowish above, with distinct yellow to orange stripe down the back.
- Strictly terrestrial, seldom venturing into trees or bushes
- Nocturnal, but may bask in the early morning or late afternoon
- Often active on overcast days

A yellowish individual

Rodents form part of this snake's diet

OLIVE SNAKE

Lycodonomorphus inornatus

Other names:
Olive House Snake,
Black House Snake,
Olyfhuisslang, Olyfslang,
Nagslang,

Average length 50–70cm

Maximum length
1.3m

HARMLESS

Widespread across southern and eastern South Africa and Eswatini. This snake prefers damp areas and is partial to rubble and rockeries as well as old logs. It is occasionally found around human dwellings, especially in the Cape and the KwaZulu-Natal Midlands. It is nocturnal and actively hunts for prey, such as geckos, rodents and other snakes. Colour is uniform olive-green, olive-grey, light brown, brownish black or black above; the underside is the same colour or slightly lighter, especially the chin, throat and forepart of the body. It is generally a docile snake, although some individuals may bite if handled, causing slight bleeding. It is sometimes confused with other uniformly coloured snakes like the harmless Brown Water Snake or the venomous Cape Cobra or Black Mamba.

This snake lacks markings on the body.

AT A GLANCE

- Uniform olive-green to grey or black above with no markings
- Relatively small eyes
- Strictly ground-living
- Active at night
- Juveniles in the west are olive-green with a darker head
- Juveniles in the east may be pitch black
- Adults may have a pale lower jaw

A very dark Olive Snake

Luke Kemp

111

BROWN WATER SNAKE

Lycodonomorphus rufulus

HARMLESS

Widespread across southern, central and eastern South Africa as well as Lesotho, Eswatini and parts of Mozambique. A separate population occurs in eastern Zimbabwe. It prefers rivers, streams, vleis and damp areas in grassland, moist savanna, lowland forest and fynbos. It is mainly nocturnal, where it may be seen climbing reeds or swimming along banks of dams in search of frogs, tadpoles, fish and occasionally geckos, lizards, birds and small rodents. It is a common snake throughout much of its range and can be found beneath rocks, logs and other debris. Zulu people traditionally believe it to be very dangerous – in fact, it is shy and harmless. Colour is uniform blackish brown to olive or light brown above; the underside ranges from mother-of-pearl white to pink, yellowish or light orange, which extends slightly up the lower sides of the body. It is a docile snake and seldom bites. May be confused with other harmless snakes, such as the Olive Snake and the Brown House Snake, or can even be mistaken for a small Black Mamba. It is distinguished by its uniform coloration and pink or orange belly.

Average length
40–60cm

Maximum length
97cm

AT A GLANCE

- Uniform blackish brown to light brown above
- Mother-of-pearl white to pink or light orange belly
- Bulging brown eyes with vertical pupils
- A good swimmer
- Elongate tail helps with swimming
- Usually found around water or damp areas
- Often seen searching between rocks under water
- Active largely at night
- Hunts frogs, tadpoles and fish

A Brown Water Snake with a pink belly

Luke Kemp

The eyes have vertical pupils.   This snake is usually blackish brown.

COMMON WOLF SNAKE

Lycophidion capense

HARMLESS

Average length
20–40cm

Maximum length
64cm

AT A GLANCE

- A small, flattened, pointed head distinct from a slender body
- Uniform brown to blackish above with white-edged scales
- Long, recurved front teeth on both jaws
- Active at night

Widespread across southern, central and eastern South Africa as well as Lesotho, Eswatini and Mozambique. Found throughout Zimbabwe, southern, eastern and northern Botswana as well as northern Namibia. A ground-living, slow-moving snake that seldom attempts to bite. It is active at night, when it hunts for lizards, especially skinks and geckos. It is fond of damp localities and is usually found under stones or logs, piles of thatch and rubbish heaps, or in deserted termite mounds. It has long, recurved front teeth on both jaws, hence the common name; these teeth allow it to hold onto slippery prey such as skinks. When threatened, it may flatten its entire body and may move in jerky movements. Colour is uniform light brown to dark brown or blackish above, typically with white-edged scales that give a speckled effect. The underside is usually white, and occasionally extends slightly up the lower sides of the body, and may have darker speckles. May be confused with other insignificant-looking snakes as well as the venomous Bibron's Stiletto Snake.

The body is uniformly light to dark brown or blackish above.

This snake has a small, flat, pointed head and a slender body. White-edged scales give it a speckled effect.

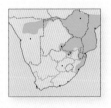

Average length
80–120cm

Maximum length
1.75m

COMMON FILE SNAKE

Limaformosa capensis

HARMLESS

Widespread across the eastern parts of South Africa, Eswatini, Mozambique and Zimbabwe. Extends through northern Botswana into northern Namibia. Although somewhat common, it is rarely seen, spending much of its time underground. It may be seen moving at night, especially after rains. It feeds on lizards, frogs and small mammals but seems particularly partial to eating other snakes, even highly venomous species. It is a very docile snake and rarely bites, even if handled. They will secrete a foul-smelling substance used for self-defence if handled. This large snake has a distinct triangular profile with a row of large, white scales down the centre of the back. Colour is grey with pink to mauve skin between the scales and a darker head. Due to its distinct profile and colours, it is seldom confused with other snakes.

The triangular body and white vertebral stripe are diagnostic features.

AT A GLANCE

- Triangular body with rough scales
- Distinctive cream to white vertebral stripe
- Light pink skin between the scales
- Fairly docile snake that rarely attempts to bite
- Nocturnal

This snake feeds mainly on other snakes. Here (right) it is seen eating an Olive Grass Snake.

Kirsty Kale

COMMON SLUG-EATER

Duberria lutrix

HARMLESS

Average length
20–35cm

Maximum length
45.2cm

AT A GLANCE

- A small head barely distinct from the rest of the body
- Distinct broad, reddish-brown band across the centre of the back
- May roll up in a tight spiral
- Has powerful scent glands, which it may use in self-defence
- Favours damp localities

Widespread across southern, eastern and central South Africa, Lesotho and western Eswatini. A common and harmless snake that favours damp localities, where it preys on snails and slugs. It is ground-living and seeks shelter under any form of cover, including rocks, logs, grass tufts and other vegetation. It is frequently found in gardens, especially in the Eastern and Western Cape provinces. This snake seldom attempts to bite; instead, it often chooses to roll up into a spiral with its head concealed, very much like a roll of tobacco, hence the Afrikaans name 'Tabakrolletjie'. It has powerful scent glands, which secrete a foul-smelling substance used for self-defence. It has a distinct broad, reddish-brown to light brown or tan band running across the centre of the back, flanked by a greyish band on either side of the body. There may be broken black dorsolateral lines. All of these markings will be barely visible in specimens about to shed. The underside is usually cream to yellowish white, edged with black or dark grey dotted lines, resulting in a light band down the centre of the belly. It may be mistaken for a young Mole Snake or juvenile Cape Cobra but does not have the same patterns or profile as either species.

It may have a reddish-brown band down the centre of the back.

It rolls up in a spiral when threatened.

The Common Slug-eater locates its prey by following a slime trail.

Tyrone Ping

115

SPOTTED BUSH SNAKE

Philothamnus semivariegatus

Average length
40–90cm

Maximum length
1.3m

Widespread through most of eastern southern Africa into parts of the Northern Cape and central Namibia. A beautifully marked, alert and active snake that moves gracefully or in short bursts if disturbed. It is diurnal and fond of basking. Colour is usually bright green to olive-green, copper or grey above with black speckles or black crossbars on the front half or two-thirds of the body. The head and neck are usually green or blue-green in colour with golden or orange to red in the eyes. This snake is an excellent climber – its keeled belly scales enable it to easily climb up the bark of trees or even brick walls. It often enters houses and outbuildings in search of geckos and frogs. Frequents riverbanks, moist savanna and lowland forest, as well as shrubs, bushes and rocky regions. Commonly found in well-vegetated gardens in KwaZulu-Natal and Limpopo. It is quick to move off if disturbed and will not hesitate to bite if handled. At night, it may sleep loosely coiled on the outer branches of trees and shrubs and will drop to the ground if disturbed. Often mistaken for a Green Mamba or the green variation of the Boomslang as well as other harmless green snakes.

AT A GLANCE

- Usually green in colour with black speckles on the front half of the body
- Round pupils with a golden or orange iris
- Bright blue tongue with a black tip
- An expert climber and can even climb up brick walls
- Often inhabits the space between walls and corrugated roofs
- Active during the day

Ashley Kemp

The front half of the body usually has black speckles or crossbars.

The round eyes have a golden or orange iris.

It is bright green or olive-green with a green or blue-green head.

Average length
70cm

Maximum length
1.2m

AT A GLANCE

- Usually quite thin with the head distinct from the body
- Bright green above with a light green or yellowish belly
- May have black spots on the neck
- Dark eyes with round pupils
- Tongue is bright blue with a black tip
- An expert climber
- Active during the day

WESTERN NATAL GREEN SNAKE

Philothamnus occidentalis

HARMLESS

The Western Natal Green Snake occurs from the Western Cape into the Eastern Cape, southern and western KwaZulu-Natal, the eastern Free State, Mpumalanga, Gauteng, Limpopo and the North West Province, as well as western Eswatini. Colour is uniform bright green, often with turquoise on the head and tail. The underside is pale greenish white or light yellowish. Juveniles may have dark crossbars on the forebody. The eye is notably dark. It is an active, alert, diurnal snake that spends most of its time in shrubs and trees. Commonly found near water and favours dense vegetation where it is very well camouflaged. It hunts for frogs and lizards. It has keeled belly scales and is a good climber, quick to escape into the surrounding vegetation if disturbed. When captured, it may inflate its neck and will bite readily. Often mistaken for a Green Mamba or the green variation of the Boomslang as well as other harmless green snakes.

The head and tail are often turquoise in colour.

The eye is notably dark.   *This snake is fond of basking.*

117

Other names:
Oostelike Natalse
Groenslang

Average length
60–80cm

Maximum length
1.3m

AT A GLANCE

- Usually quite thin with the head distinct from the body
- Bright green above with a light green or yellowish belly
- May have black spots on the neck
- Black eyes with yellow irises and round pupils
- Tongue is bright blue with black tip
- An expert climber
- Active during the day

EASTERN NATAL GREEN SNAKE

Philothamnus natalensis

HARMLESS

The Eastern Natal Green Snake occurs from Amanzimtoti in KwaZulu-Natal, northwards along the east of KwaZulu-Natal, to Mpumalanga and Limpopo, as well as Mozambique, eastern Eswatini and Zimbabwe. Colour is uniform bright green, often with some yellow and sometimes with dark bars on the neck. The underside is pale green or light yellowish. The eye has a bright yellow iris. It is an active, alert, diurnal snake that spends most of its time in shrubs and trees. Commonly found around houses, especially basking on boardwalks and decks. It hunts for frogs and lizards. It is a good climber, quick to escape into the surrounding vegetation if disturbed. When captured, it may inflate its neck and will bite readily. Often mistaken for a Green Mamba or the green variation of the Boomslang as well as other harmless green snakes.

The Eastern Natal Green Snake is often mistaken for a Green Mamba.

This snake occurs mostly in trees or shrubs.

The eyes are black with yellow irises and round pupils.

Average length 30–50cm

Maximum length 1m

AT A GLANCE

- Bright emerald green above, with a pale yellow snout
- White or yellow belly
- Round pupils
- May have dark blotches on the neck in Mozambique
- Very good swimmer
- Slow-moving and docile
- Diurnal
- May sleep curled up in reeds or under logs and rocks

GREEN WATER SNAKE

Philothamnus hoplogaster

HARMLESS

Widespread through eastern South Africa, Eswatini, Mozambique and Zimbabwe. Colour is uniform bright green, usually with a light yellow snout. In the northern parts of the range there may be dark blotches on the neck. Underside is white or light yellowish to cream. It is an active, alert, diurnal snake that favours damp localities such as reed swamps, riverine thickets and floodplains. It is an excellent swimmer but will also climb trees and shrubs. It hunts for frogs and lizards and reportedly fish. It is a docile snake, seldom attempting to bite. Often mistaken for a Green Mamba or the green variation of the Boomslang as well as other harmless green snakes.

The Green Water Snake occurs in the east and northeast of the region.

This snake's snout is often pale yellow.

119

Average length
40–60cm

Maximum length
1.16m

COMMON EGG-EATER
Dasypeltis scabra

HARMLESS

Found across most of southern Africa. Largely absent from the Kalahari Desert and the sandy west coast of Namibia. A common snake in dry thornveld, fynbos and grasslands where it may be found hiding under logs and rocks during the day or active at night. When agitated, it will coil and uncoil, creating a hissing sound with the rough scales. It will also strike out quite viciously with its mouth wide open, exposing the dark inner lining of the mouth. Its diet consists of bird eggs, so the teeth serve no purpose and are greatly reduced. Colour is variable from light brown to grey-brown, dark brown or reddish above, with a series of dark brown rhombic markings down the back, and narrow, dark brown bars down either side of the body. A V-shaped marking on the nape is usually preceded by two similar, but narrower markings on the head. The underside is white, sometimes with dark spots and flecks. Uniform brown individuals with virtually no markings occur quite frequently. It is easily confused with the Common Night Adder and the Horned Adder.

AT A GLANCE

- Dark brown rhombic markings on the back
- One or more V-shaped markings on the head and nape
- The inside of the mouth and the tongue are black
- Vertical pupils
- Active at night

The inside of the mouth and the tongue are black.

Coiled in defensive pose

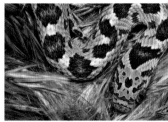

It may have V-markings on its neck.

BROWN EGG-EATER

Dasypeltis inornata

Average length 50–70cm

Maximum length 1.2m

HARMLESS

Found in eastern South Africa as well as western Eswatini. It may be common in much of its range and is often found in gardens on the south coast of KwaZulu-Natal. It is nocturnal, spending most of the day in hiding beneath logs and rocks. The Brown Egg-eater seldom performs the defense display of the Common Egg-eater. Its diet consists of bird eggs, so the teeth serve no purpose and are greatly reduced. Colour is grey, olive, brown to reddish brown without any other markings and with distinct rough keeled scales. The lower sides are often light yellowish. The underside is white to pale yellowish. It is a docile snake and is easily confused with other uniform-coloured snakes and the plain form of the Common Egg-eater.

The body is uniform yellowish red to brown above with a pale belly.

AT A GLANCE

- Small head, barely discernible from neck
- Vertical pupils
- Uniform yellowish red to reddish brown above
- Underside is cream to white
- Keeled scales give it a rough appearance
- Red to orange tongue
- Pink mouth lining
- Nocturnal
- Often climbs trees to raid birds' nests

The tongue is orange to red.

This snake is a good climber.

121

Other names:
Schlegel se Blindeslang

Average length
40–60cm

Maximum length
90cm

AT A GLANCE

- Medium to large with a cylindrical body
- Beaked snout
- Varies in patterning from plain to blotched or striped
- Small, dark eyes are prominent
- Has a spike on the tip of the tail
- Lives underground
- Sometimes seen moving or crossing roads, usually after heavy rain

SCHLEGEL'S BLIND SNAKE

Afrotyphlops schlegelii

HARMLESS

Found in eastern South Africa as well as western Eswatini and southern Mozambique. Extends into central and northern Botswana into northern Namibia. It spends much of its life underground and in termite mounds, but is commonly seen in gardens or crossing roads after heavy rains. Colour is variable and is usually light blue to grey or brown with dark blotches and pale speckles. The tail is rounded and sometimes confused with the head. The head has a strong beak on the snout and a small eye spot. It hunts termites and the eggs, often digging into termite mounds in search of the egg chambers. It is a harmless, docile snake, but if handled may emit a foul-smelling liquid and will press the sharp-tipped tail into the handler. This may give the handler a fright but will not cause any harm. It is easily confused with other blind snakes like the Zambezi Blind snake.

Coloration varies from light blue or grey to brown or beige.

Note the large rostral shield for burrowing.

An individual that has just shed its skin

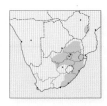

BIBRON'S BLIND SNAKE
Afrotyphlops bibronii

HARMLESS

Found in eastern South Africa as well as Eswatini and eastern Zimbabwe. It spends much of its life underground and under logs and rocks but may be seen moving after heavy rains. It may be found in small groups beneath rocks or logs. It is also occasionally dug up in garden beds and often falls into swimming pools. Colour is reddish brown to purplish, brown, pink or light grey. The tail is rounded and sometimes confused with the head. The head has a strong beak on the snout and a small eye spot. It hunts termites and ants and their eggs and larvae. It is a harmless, docile snake, but if handled may emit a foul-smelling liquid and will press the sharp-tipped tail into the handler. This may give the handler a fright but will not cause any harm. It is easily confused with other blind snakes like Delalande's Beaked Blind Snake as well as the venomous Bibron's Stiletto Snake. It is often incorrectly referred to as a Mole Snake.

Average length 20–35cm
Maximum length 48.4cm

Bibron's Blind Snake is shiny dark to olive-brown above.

AT A GLANCE

- Shiny dark brown to olive-brown above, with a paler belly
- Very prominent snout
- Small, dark eyes and a small, pink tongue
- Fossorial and seldom seen on the surface
- Sometimes found after rains or in swimming pools

This snake has tiny eyes and a prominent rostral shield.

Fossorial, it is seldom seen on the surface, except after heavy rains.

123

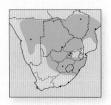

PETERS' THREAD SNAKE

Leptotyphlops scutifrons scutifrons

Average length
15–20cm

Maximum length
28cm

AT A GLANCE

- Slender, with a cylindrical body
- Uniform red-brown to black
- Scales are highly polished
- Tail ends in a spine
- Found in a variety of habitats from forest to Karoo scrub

HARMLESS

Found across much of northern and central southern Africa. Absent from the southwestern regions of southern Africa as well as southern Mozambique. It is common in much of its range but seldom seen as it lives underground and under logs and rocks as well as in thick leaf litter. It is occasionally found after heavy rains or is dug up while gardening or during earth works. Colour is dark brown to black with large, polished scales. Its diet consists of termites and ants and their eggs and larvae. It is a harmless snake but will wriggle wildly if handled and has been reported to play dead if handled in a rough manner. It is easily confused with other harmless thread snakes.

The scales may be pale-edged, giving the body a chequered pattern.

This snake feeds on invertebrates.

If handled roughly, it may pretend to be dead.

GLOSSARY

Anal Of or near the anus

Anaphylaxis A severe allergic reaction to an allergen, usually a protein. It is rapid and may result in lowered blood pressure, closing up of the throat, and could lead to cardiac arrest.

Anterior Situated at or near the front

Antivenom Serum produced from the antibodies of animals, which is used to combat the effects of venom

Aquatic Living in or near water

Clutch (eggs) A group of eggs fertilised and laid at one time

Cryptic Hidden or camouflaged to resemble the environment, e.g., the coloration of the Vine Snake mimics a branch or twig.

Cytotoxic (venom) Adversely affecting tissue and cell formation. The venom of adders and spitting cobras is predominantly cytotoxic.

Diurnal Active mainly during the day

Dorsal Pertaining to the upper surface of the body

Elapids Snakes of the family Elapidae, such as cobras and mambas, which are characterised by jawbones that are incapable of marked rotation – their fangs are therefore erect at all times.

Endemic Limited to a particular geographic region. A species is classified as endemic if more than 90% of its distribution records come from within a specific area.

Fang A large, specialised tooth adapted for the injection of venom; usually hollow, but sometimes grooved in the front

Fossorial Adapted to burrowing and living below ground

Haemotoxic (venom) Adversely affecting the blood-clotting mechanism, causing severe bleeding from the mucous membranes and, eventually, bleeding from other organs. The venom of the Boomslang and the Vine Snake is predominantly haemotoxic.

Hatchling A newborn reptile produced by an egg-laying species

Keel (snakes) A ridge on the scales of some snakes, e.g., the Boomslang and the Rinkhals

Lymph A colourless, alkaline fluid circulated around the body by the lymphatic system

Monovalent (antivenom) An antivenom that is effective against one type of venom

Montane Pertaining to mountains

Necrosis The death of cells in an organ or tissue, usually within a localised area

Neurotoxic (venom) Adversely affecting neuromuscular function. The venom of mambas and some cobras, e.g., the Cape Cobra, is predominantly neurotoxic.

Nocturnal Active mainly at night

Oviparous Egg-laying

Polyvalent (antivenom) An antivenom that is effective against several different venoms at the same time

Recurved Curved backwards

Rhombic With four sides of equal length, diamond-shaped

Riverine Pertaining to an area in or near a river

Subocular (scales) A scale that separates the eye from scales on the upper lip

Terrestrial Ground-living

Viviparous Giving birth to live young

FURTHER READING

www.africansnakebiteinstitute.com

Alexander, G. & Marais, J. 2007. *A Guide to the Reptiles of Southern Africa*. Struik Nature, Cape Town, South Africa.

Branch, B. 1998. *Field Guide to Snakes and other Reptiles of Southern Africa*. Struik Nature, Cape Town, South Africa.

Marais, J. 2022. *A Complete Guide to Snakes of Southern Africa*. Struik Nature, Cape Town, South Africa.

Marais, J. 2007. *What's that Snake?* Struik Nature, Cape Town, South Africa.

Marais, J. 2011. *What's that Reptile?* Struik Nature, Cape Town, South Africa.

INDEX

Key: **Common name** Alternative English common name *Scientific name*

A
Adder
  Berg 32
  Bibron's Burrowing 85
  Cape Berg 32
  Common Night 40
  Drakensberg Berg 32
  Gaboon 29
  Horned 35
  Many-horned 38
  Puff 26
  Rhombic Night 40
  Southern Burrowing 85
  Zimbabwe Berg 32
Adders 25
Afrotyphlops bibronii 123
Afrotyphlops schlegelii 122
Aspidelaps lubricus cowlesi 72
Aspidelaps lubricus lubricus 70
Aspidelaps scutatus scutatus 74
Atractaspis bibronii 85
B
Back-fanged snakes 78
Bird Snake 82
Bitis arietans arietans 26
Bitis atropos 32
Bitis caudalis 35
Bitis cornuta 38
Bitis gabonica 29

Black Snake
  Natal 88
Blind Snake
  Bibron's 123
  Schlegel's 122
Boaedon capensis 109
Boomslang 79
  Cape 79
  Common 79
Burrowing Asp 85
Bush Snake
  Spotted 116
  Variegated 116
C
Causus rhombeatus 40
Cobra
  Anchieta's 54
  Banded 52
  Black-necked Spitting 60
  Black Spitting 58
  Brown Forest 56
  Cape 49
  Eastern Shield-nose 72
  Egyptian 52
  Kunene Shield 72
  Mozambique Spitting 64
  Shield-nose 74
  Snouted 52
  Western Barred Spitting 62
  Zebra 62

Coral Snake 70
  Angolan 72
  Cape 70
  Kunene 72
  Western 72
Crotaphopeltis hotamboeia 100
D
Dasypeltis inornata 121
Dasypeltis scabra 120
Dendroaspis angusticeps 46
Dendroaspis polylepis 43
Dispholidus typus 79
Dispholidus typus typus 79
Dispholidus typus viridis 79
Duberria lutrix 115
E
Egg-eater
  Brown 121
  Common 120
  Rhombic 120
  Southern Brown 121
Elapids 42
Elapsoidea boulengeri 76
F
Fangless snakes 108
File Snake
  Cape 114
  Common 114

Olive Snake

G
Garter Snake
  Boulenger's 76
  Zambezi 76
Grass Snake
  Olive 90
  Short-snouted 92
  Spotted 96
Green Snake
  Eastern Natal 118
  Southeastern 119
  Water 119
  Western Natal 117
H
Hemachatus haemachatus 67
Herald Snake 100
House Snake
  Aurora 110
  Black 111
  Brown 109
  Olive 111
L
Lamprophis aurora 110
Leptotyphlops scutifrons scutifrons 124
Limaformosa capensis 114
Lycodonomorphus inornatus 111
Lycodonomorphus rufulus 112
Lycophidion capense 113
M
Macrelaps microlepidotus 88
Mamba
  Black 43
  Black-mouthed 43
  Green 46
Mole Snake 106

N
Naja anchietae 54
Naja annulifera 52
Naja mossambica 64
Naja nigricincta nigricincta 62
Naja nigricincta woodi 58
Naja nigricollis 60
Naja nivea 49
Naja subfulva 56
Non-venomous snakes 108
O
Olive Snake 111
P
Peters' Worm Snake 124
Philothamnus hoplogaster 119
Philothamnus natalensis 118
Philothamnus occidentalis 117
Philothamnus semivariegatus 116
Psammophis brevirostris 92
Psammophis mossambicus 90
Psammophis subtaeniatus 94
Psammophylax rhombeatus 96
Pseudaspis cana 106
Python
  African Rock 103
  Southern African 103
Python natalensis 103
R
Rinkhals 67
S
Sand Snake
  Olive 90
  Short-snouted 92
  Stripe-bellied 94
  Western Yellow-bellied 94
Shield-nose Snake 74
  Speckled 74

Skaapsteker
  Spotted 96
  Rhombic 96
Slug-eater
  Common 115
  South African 115
Speckled Shield-nose Snake 74
Stiletto Snake
  Bibron's 85
T
Telescopus semiannulatus 98
Thelotornis capensis 82
Thelotornis capensis capensis 82
Thelotornis capensis oatesii 82
Thelotornis mossambicanus 82
Thread Snake
  Peters' 124
Tiger Snake
  Eastern 98
Tree Snake 79
Twig Snake 82
V
Vine Snake
  Eastern 82
  Oates' 82
  Southern 82
W
Water Snake
  Brown 112
Whip Snake
  Olive 90
  Short-snouted 92
Wolf Snake
  Cape 113
  Common 113
Worm Snake
  Peters' 124

Spotted Skaapsteker

ACKNOWLEDGEMENTS

Many people have contributed to this book – far too many to mention. Herpetology is a strange addiction, and one gets to deal with a weird mix of people who are most passionate about their interests and very willing to share their time and knowledge. I have been privileged to spend a lot of time with Paul Moler, Randy Babb, Luke Kemp, Aaron Bauer, the late Bill Branch, Graham Alexander, the late Gordon Setaro, the late Wulf Haacke, and the late Don Broadley, from whom I have learnt a great deal. On the subject of snakebite, I have had endless discussions with Dr Colin Tilbury, Dr Gerbus Muller, Dr David Warrell, Dr George Oosthuizen and Jason Seale, and have also gained invaluable information from various technical publications on the subject. I would also like to thank the African Snakebite team, especially Ashley Kemp and Luke Kemp, for all their help and advice. Both Paul Moler and Luke Kemp read through the text and corrected errors and suggested improvements. I happily take responsibility for any remaining errors.

Several people have made snakes available to photograph and, unfortunately, it is not possible to acknowledge all of them. Reptile photographers generously shared their images and are acknowledged next to their photographs.

My thanks to my good friend and colleague Luke Kemp who has put a great deal of time and effort into this book, shared his photographs and provided the distribution maps and Struik Nature Publishers, especially Pippa Parker. We have had a great working relationship for many years.

Lastly, my thanks to all the passionate snake enthusiasts who have contributed greatly to public education about these fascinating creatures. I have seen people's attitudes towards snakes changing over the past 45 years and have no doubt that we are making excellent progress in our conservation endeavours. This book is dedicated to my daughter, Melissa, whom I love dearly.

Green Mamba